BY AMY NATHAN

COUNT ON US

AMERICAN WOMEN IN THE MILITARY

FOREWORD BY
WALTER CRONKITE

355
JN

NATIONAL GEOGRAPHIC SOCIETY
Washington, D.C.

**Dedicated to the women of the armed forces
of the United States**

Book design by David M. Seager

Text type is Minion; display type is Eagle Bold, House Broken Clean, and Trade Gothic Bold Condensed

Library of Congress Cataloging-in-Publication Data available on request.

ISBN: 0-7922-6330-8

One of the world's largest nonprofit scientific and educational organizations, the National Geographic Society was founded in 1888 "for the increase and diffusion of geographic knowledge." Fulfilling this mission, the Society educates and inspires millions every day through its magazines, books, television programs, videos, maps and atlases, research grants, the National Geographic Bee, teacher workshops, and innovative classroom materials. The Society is supported through membership dues, charitable gifts, and income from the sale of its educational products. This support is vital to National Geographic's mission to increase global understanding and promote conservation of our planet through exploration, research, and education.

For more information, please call 1-800-NGS-LINE (647-5463) or write to the following address:

National Geographic Society
1145 17th Street N.W.
Washington, D.C. 20036-4688
U.S.A.

Visit the Society's Web site: www.nationalgeographic.com

Printed in Belgium

Published by the National Geographic Society

John M. Fahey, Jr., *President and Chief Executive Officer*

Gilbert M. Grosvenor, *Chairman of the Board*

Nina D. Hoffman, *Executive Vice President,
President of Books and Education Publishing Group*

Ericka Markman, *Senior Vice President, President of Children's Books
and Education Publishing Group*

Staff for this book

Nancy Laties Feresten,
Vice President, Editor-in-Chief, Children's Books

Bea Jackson, *Art Director, Children's Books*

Suzanne Patrick Fonda, *Project Editor*

Janet Dustin, *Illustrations Editor*

Jennifer Emmett, *Editor*

Marfé Ferguson-Delano, *Editor*

Judith Klein, *Copy Editor*

Julia Marshall, *Indexer*

R. Gary Colbert, *Production Director*

Lewis R. Bassford, *Production Manager*

Vincent P. Ryan, *Manager, Manufacturing and Quality Control*

Photo Credits

Front cover, © Swim Ink/CORBIS; title page, 62, 68–9 both, 72, back cover, courtesy Defense Visual Information Center, Department of Defense; 4, 16, 18, 20, 24, 26, 27, 28, 30–31, 33 up, 36, 44, 48, 50, 52 courtesy National Archives; 5 © Bettmann/CORBIS; 6 courtesy Marshall Karesh, Convention Photography Services, Inc.; 8, 11, 12 Louis S. Glanzman, National Geographic Society; 10 © 2002 James Singewald; 13 © 2002 Carl Nathan; 14 courtesy U.S. Army Military History Institute; 17 from *Women's Work in the Civil War*, by Linus P. Brockett and Mary C. Vaughan, Philadelphia: Zeigler, McCurdy, 1867; 19 courtesy Schomburg Center for Research in Black Culture, New York Public Library; 21 courtesy Lauren Cook Wike; 23 courtesy Women In Military Service For America Memorial Foundation, Inc., Rose M. Heavren Collection; 29 courtesy Oberlin College Archives, Oberlin, OH; 32, 42, 54, 56 Army Nurse Corps Collection, Office of Medical History, Office of the U.S. Surgeon General; 33 lo courtesy Armed Forces Institute of Pathology; 34 courtesy Kautz Family YMCA Archives, YMCA of the USA; 38 courtesy Irene Brion; 39 courtesy United States Air Force Museum; 40 courtesy U.S. Army Signal Corps; 41 courtesy Naval Historical Center; 43 courtesy Dorothy Steinbis Davis; 45 courtesy Bureau of Medicine and Surgery, Department of the Navy; 46 courtesy Helen P. Richardson; 51 courtesy Carmela Filosa Hix; 53 courtesy Ernestine Johnson Thomas; 57 courtesy Lily Lee Adams; 58 courtesy Julia Barnes; 59 courtesy U.S. Coast Guard; 60 courtesy Theresa Nguyen; 61, 85 courtesy U.S. Army; 64 courtesy Christina Richter Listermann; 65 courtesy Celia FlorCruz; 66 both courtesy Mary Fowlkes; 67 courtesy Kim Chambers; 70 courtesy Army Times Publishing Company; 71 courtesy Susan Fink; 74 courtesy Kristen Fabry; 75 courtesy Christine Knighton; 76 courtesy Anita Dixon; 77 courtesy Women In Military Service For America Memorial Foundation, Inc., Cynthia A. Pritchett Collection; 78 courtesy U.S. Marine Corps; 80 le courtesy Elizabeth Dunn; 80rt © Robert Patrick/CORBIS SYGMA; 82 courtesy Rudy Gutierrez, *El Paso Times*; 83 courtesy Linda Stelter, *El Paso Times*.

Front cover: Painting of a female Marine from a World War II Marine recruiting poster

Back cover: Marine recruit at M-16A1 rifle practice during basic training

Title page: A Marine recruit during basic training. The Marine Corps is the only branch of the service that still has women go through basic training in all-female battalions. In the other branches of the armed forces, men and women go through basic training in mixed-gender units.

Note: Throughout the book, servicewomen are identified wherever possible using the highest rank they achieved.

THESE U.S. ARMY WOMEN ARE ARRIVING TO SERVE IN
AUSTRALIA IN 1944, DURING WORLD WAR II. ABOUT
350,000 WOMEN SERVED IN THE ARMED FORCES OF THE
UNITED STATES DURING WORLD WAR II. THEY PERFORMED
A MUCH WIDER RANGE OF MILITARY JOBS THAN WOMEN
HAD BEEN ALLOWED TO DO BEFORE. IN CHAPTER 4 YOU
CAN LEARN MORE ABOUT THEM.

FOREWORD

BY WALTER CRONKITE

As a young newspaper reporter in the 1940s, I was out there on the periphery of history as women finally were officially given new expanded roles to play in the military forces of the United States. So important was that development that I have always been proud that I had some partial connection to it.

Before then, military women had been allowed mainly to nurse the wounded and, during World War I, to help with the office work. But all that changed in December 1941 when the Japanese attacked Pearl Harbor. The United States was plunged into World War II, but it was ill prepared for the all-out mobilization of military forces that was required. Within six months the realization struck Washington that there was a vast pool of women who were anxious and willing to actively participate in the fight ahead.

I knew the woman who was put in charge of the newly established Women's Army Auxiliary Corps, the WAACs. She was Oveta Culp Hobby, and she and her husband owned the *Houston Post,* where I had my first newspaper job in the late 1930s. She had treated this cub reporter kindly, and, from a great distance, I developed a great admiration for her. With Mrs. Hobby in charge, I put any male chauvinism behind me and knew that the WAACs would make a major contribution to our war effort. That was not a universally held opinion at that time: Skeptics had a field day of doubt before Congress established the Corps in 1942.

Colonel Hobby began to recruit her first volunteers, and here again I was touched by history. The first five or six women in the New York City area chosen for officer training were introduced at a press conference, and I was one of the lucky young men who had a chance to admire these outstanding women in their snappy new uniforms. Thus the United Press carried around the world my interview with one of these pioneers helping to make military history.

Throughout World War II in North Africa and Europe, I was privileged to see our military women performing their assigned roles in combat areas. Over television, I reported on their roles in later wars, in Korea, Vietnam, and then their appearance flying support missions in the first Persian Gulf War. Those reports included, sadly, one about a young woman pilot killed in action.

Our women in uniform continued to make history in the recent Iraq war. We can share in their pride and count on them as part of our armed forces deep into our future.

Walter Cronkite (above), one of the most respected figures in news reporting, was a newspaper reporter during World War II. After the war, he was managing editor and anchor on the CBS Evening News for many years. He continues to host news and documentary programs on various television networks.

ON OCTOBER 18, 1997, PEOPLE GATHERED FOR THE DEDICATION CEREMONY OF THE WOMEN IN MILITARY SERVICE FOR AMERICA MEMORIAL. A GROUP OF MILITARY WOMEN WORKED FOR MORE THAN TEN YEARS, FIRST TO CONVINCE THE GOVERNMENT THAT THERE SHOULD BE A MEMORIAL AND THEN TO RAISE THE MONEY TO BUILD IT. IN A SPEECH GIVEN THAT DAY, FRIEDA MAE HARDIN, WHO SERVED IN THE NAVY IN WORLD WAR I, TOLD THE CROWD, "IN MY 101 YEARS OF LIVING, I HAVE OBSERVED MANY WONDERFUL ACHIEVEMENTS—BUT NONE AS IMPORTANT OR AS MEANINGFUL AS THE PROGRESS OF WOMEN IN TAKING THEIR RIGHTFUL PLACE IN SOCIETY. WHEN I SERVED IN THE NAVY, WOMEN WERE NOT EVEN ALLOWED TO VOTE!"

REMEMBERED AT LAST

"When I saw all the women who were there, I got a lump in my throat and my eyes filled with tears. I thought of the saying 'You've come a long way, baby.'" That's what went through the mind of Command Sergeant Major Cynthia Pritchett on a chilly October day in 1997 as she stood with 40,000 people at the gateway to Arlington National Cemetery. This landmark near Washington, D.C., is where many men and women who served in the armed forces of the United States are buried. A new building was being dedicated there that day: the Women In Military Service For America Memorial, known as the Women's Memorial. This was the first memorial to honor all of the nearly two million women who have volunteered to serve with the U.S. armed forces throughout the nation's history.

It was an emotional day. For many years, women's contributions had not been noticed much, either in national monuments or in history books. This was especially true for women who pitched in to help whenever the nation was at war. Not only had women in the military been ignored by history, but they often had trouble being allowed even to serve. For a long time, most people thought the military should be only for men.

However, there have always been gutsy women who were determined to help in wartime, no matter what. Women have taken part in every major war in the nation's history, starting with the Revolutionary War that led to the birth of the nation more than 200 years ago. Women served well in all those wars, earning praise from male commanders and medals for bravery. As Colonel Mary Hallaren said when she signed up in the 1940s to help with World War II, "You don't have to be six foot and male to have a brain and know how to use it."

When Command Sergeant Major Pritchett looked at the crowd at the dedication ceremony for the Women's Memorial, she saw many older women. Some had served during World War II. There were a few who had served in World War I, nearly 80 years before. Things were tough for military women back then. She was grateful to these older women for having the courage to lead the way. Also in the crowd were younger women, who, like her, were currently in the armed forces, serving at a time when women were accepted, finally, as members of the force.

This book takes a look at the contributions made by servicewomen, past and present. These women all volunteered to serve—they did not have to be in the military, as so many men did in past years when there was something called the "draft," which required men to sign up and serve if needed. However, this is not only a story about the military. The struggle to open opportunities for women in the armed forces is an important part of women's history.

There is a quote carved into a skylight at the Women's Memorial that sums up the feelings of many servicewomen. It comes from Major Beatrice Hood Stroup, who served with the Army in World War II. She said, "It isn't just my brother's country or my husband's country, it's my country as well. And so the war wasn't just their war, it was my war, and I needed to serve in it."

THERE ARE NO PHOTO-
GRAPHS OF WOMEN
SERVING DURING THE
REVOLUTIONARY WAR
BECAUSE CAMERAS HAD
NOT BEEN INVENTED YET.
THIS IS AN ARTIST'S
IDEA OF WHAT DEBORAH
SAMSON MIGHT HAVE
LOOKED LIKE IN
HER UNIFORM.

REVOLUTIONARY WAR

1775 - 1783

Women were part of the action right from the start. More than 200 years ago, when the 13 American Colonies fought the Revolutionary War to win their freedom from Great Britain, women were there, helping to bring about the birth of a new nation: the United States. Some pitched in to help on battlefields. Others stayed home, making clothes and ammunition for the troops. In addition to running the family farm for husbands who were away fighting, women also did some spying. As a British officer noted, "Destroy all the men in America and we shall still have all we can do to defeat the women."

A few women took part in the actual fighting, as soldiers. That was very unusual. Back then most women, other than those who were slaves, were expected to stay home and take care of their households. Most schools were closed to girls. Only a few women had paying jobs. Women could not even own property. Becoming a soldier was definitely not allowed. That did not stop Deborah Samson.

She was used to hard work, having grown up as a servant girl doing chores on a Massachusetts farm. When she was about 20 years old, the Revolutionary War had been raging for several years. The American forces needed more soldiers. She figured she was strong enough to be a soldier and earn a soldier's pay. She made a man's outfit, put it on, cut her hair, and headed to a nearby town to sign up. She did such a good job of disguising herself as a man that nobody noticed anything wrong when she signed the military registration book with a man's name: Robert Shurtlieff.

"A new scene and a new world opened to my view," she said later in a speech she gave about her wartime service. For more than a year, she fought bravely alongside the men in her battalion. They called her "Bob." When she was wounded, she did not let anyone examine her too carefully. She did not want a doctor to discover her secret. However, she finally became sick with such a high fever that she was too weak to keep a doctor from reaching inside her jacket to check for a heartbeat. Imagine his surprise when he found that "Bob" was a woman. That ended her fighting days. After she recovered from the fever, her commander gave her an honorable discharge and sent her home.

Back home in Massachusetts, people were shocked by what she had done. But she was proud of having put on the uniform "of the warrior, already prepared for battle." As she said later, "Thus I became an actor in that important drama."

SOLDIER-IN-DISGUISE

What Deborah Samson did was so unusual that it fired up the imaginations of writers back then. It is hard to know which of the many tales written about her are true. There is even disagreement about her name. Some people say it is "Sampson," with a "p," although many experts think there was no "p."

She was born in Massachusetts in 1760, near where her Pilgrim ancestors landed 140 years before. Her family was so poor that from about age 10 until her late teens she was a servant on another family's farm. The boys in that family went to school. She had them teach her to read because, like most girls then, she did not have much chance to go to school herself. At about age 18, she became a teacher in a nearby school. Then she decided to be a soldier-in-disguise. She was able to get away with pretending to be a male soldier because doctors did not examine new soldiers back then as they do today. Soldiers also did not take many baths or undress at night. They slept in their uniforms. Not shaving would not be a giveaway either because many soldiers were young boys who did not shave yet.

After her secret was discovered and she had to go home, she married a farmer and had three children. About 20 years after the war, she set out on a lecture tour, the first American woman to do so. She traveled around the Northeast delighting audiences with stories of her soldier days and demonstrations of how a soldier handles a weapon.

ON THE BATTLEFIELD

During the Revolutionary War, only a few women are said to have done what Deborah Samson did. However, thousands of others helped on the battlefield without dressing as men. They cooked for the soldiers, washed clothes, and did other chores to keep the troops ready to fight. During battles, as cannons boomed, many women risked their lives to bring water, food, and supplies to soldiers as they fought.

In emergencies, some of these women helped with weapons, including a Native-American woman named Tyonajanegen. She was a member of an Oneida tribe that fought in 1777 on the side of the Americans at Oriskany, New York. When her husband was shot in the wrist, she loaded his gun for him. A newspaper report at the time noted that she was on horseback and "fought by his side, with pistols, during the whole action, which lasted six hours." A year earlier, another woman, Margaret Corbin, was with her husband at the Battle of Fort Washington, also in New York. When her husband died in this battle, 25-year-old Captain Molly, as she was called, fired his cannon until she was wounded. The Americans lost that battle. She was taken prisoner but was soon released. Three years later, the government agreed to pay her a small amount of money for the rest of her life as a pension, like injured soldiers received. She was the first woman to earn such a pension. About 20 years after the Revolution ended, Deborah Samson received a pension, too.

Like Captain Molly, many women who traveled with the troops were soldiers' wives. When husbands signed up, wives often went along, sometimes even bringing their children. Many women did this to help the cause of freedom or to have an adventure. Others did it to survive. With a husband away fighting, women who were not wealthy or whose families did not own a farm might have a hard time supporting themselves. By traveling with the soldiers, a woman would at least have something to eat. Officials provided food for three to six women helpers for each company of troops and paid some others to care for the wounded.

Jemima Warner was one of the first women to die in the war. She went with her husband when his battalion joined others heading to Canada in the winter of 1775. They were part of an unsuccessful effort to defeat the British in Quebec. Her husband died on the way north, but she kept going, carrying his rifle. When they reached Quebec and fighting started, an enemy bullet killed her on December 11, 1775.

Historians estimate that there may have been as many as 20,000 female battlefield helpers in the Revolutionary War. There is no way to know for sure. Recordkeeping was not good back then, especially for African Americans. There are a few reports of black women serving as battlefield helpers, but it is likely that many of the wives of the more than 5,000 black men who fought with the American forces went along with their husbands.

General George Washington, commander in chief of America's Continental Army, needed women's help because he never had enough soldiers. By having women do a lot of the support work, he could free up soldiers for fighting. In later wars, too, the military would count on women to take over noncombat jobs so more men would be available to do the fighting.

IN ADDITION TO "CAPTAIN MOLLY" (MARGARET) CORBIN, ANOTHER WOMAN NICK-
NAMED MOLLY IS SAID TO HAVE HELPED SHOOT HER HUSBAND'S CANNON. HE WAS
INJURED AT THE BATTLE OF MONMOUTH IN NEW JERSEY IN 1778. EARLIER IN THE
BATTLE, SHE BROUGHT SOLDIERS PITCHERS OF WATER, EARNING HER THE NICKNAME
"MOLLY PITCHER." THE WATER WAS MAINLY FOR WASHING AND COOLING THE
CANNONS AFTER THEY WERE FIRED. IF A CANNON WAS TOO HOT, THE NEXT BATCH
OF GUNPOWDER MIGHT EXPLODE TOO SOON. SOME SAY THIS WOMAN MAY HAVE BEEN
MARY HAYS MCCAULEY. OTHERS SAY THERE ARE NOT ENOUGH RECORDS TO PROVE
SHE DID WHAT THE LEGEND SAYS MOLLY PITCHER DID.

ON THE HOME FRONT

Women who stayed home also helped. Battles took place all around them, sometimes even in their own yards. Women often picked up guns to defend their families. When some Tories—colonists who sided with the British—burst into Nancy Hart's cabin while her husband was working in the fields, she shot one and captured the others. Women also took over jobs that used to be done by men who went off to fight, something that happened in later wars, too. At that time, most people lived on farms. Men generally did the heavy, outdoor chores. With husbands gone, many wives took over those chores, along with all the other tasks they were already doing. These busy women still found time to help with the war by sewing soldiers' uniforms or melting lead spoons to make bullets. Some let their homes be used as hospitals for the wounded. Others were spies, keeping their ears open when they came in contact with British officials and passing along to American forces any military information they heard. Elizabeth Jackson, a poor widow, was one of many who took food and clothes to soldiers held prisoner by the British. While visiting a prison ship in South Carolina, she caught yellow fever, which was killing many prisoners. It killed her, too, making her teenage son Andrew an orphan. Later, he became the seventh President of the United States.

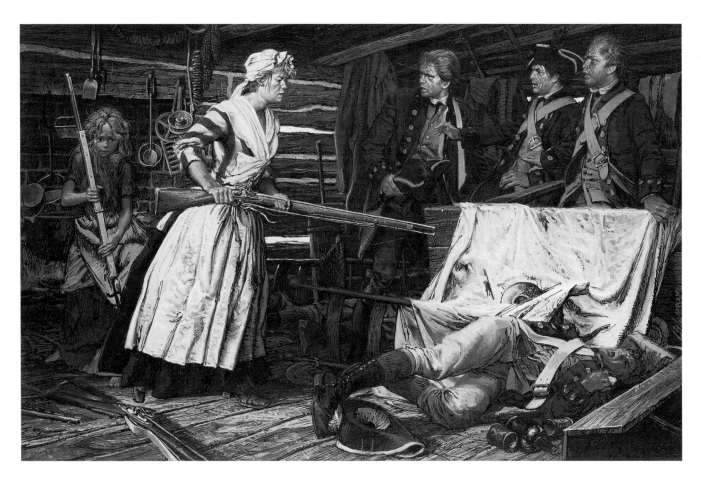

THIS IS AN ARTIST'S IDEA OF HOW NANCY HART LOOKED AFTER SHE MANAGED TO GET HOLD OF ONE OF THE RIFLES BELONGING TO SOME TORY SOLDIERS WHO ENTERED HER GEORGIA CABIN, DEMANDING FOOD. LEFT TO FEND FOR HERSELF WHILE HER HUSBAND WAS IN THE FIELDS, SHE SHOT ONE SOLDIER AND CAPTURED THE OTHERS.

SYBIL LUDINGTON

There were a few "female Paul Reveres" who rode on horseback, as Revere did, to warn people about British attacks. One of these daring messengers was 16-year-old Sybil Ludington, from New York State. On the night of April 26, 1777, she rode her horse, Star, through the countryside to round up members of her father's military unit because British troops were burning the nearby town of Danbury in Connecticut. She and Star rode all night long, through the rain, covering almost 40 miles. This was more than twice as far as Paul Revere went during his famous ride in Massachusetts two years earlier. This statue of her and Star is in a lakeside park in Carmel, New York, one of the towns this teenager rode through on that rainy spring night.

A NEW NATION

After the British surrendered in 1781 and the peace treaty was finally signed in 1783, women hoped the new U.S. government would reward them for helping win the war by giving women equal rights with men. That didn't happen. Women would not become full citizens with the right to vote in all elections for more than 130 years. But some things did change. Towns began to let more white girls go to school. This was done partly so they could become good mothers for the new nation, better able to raise children who would be responsible citizens. The job of elementary school teacher came to be seen more and more as one that was all right for women to do. Some schools hired women because they didn't have to pay them as much as they did male teachers. However, one thing did not change: Women continued to be ready to serve the nation whenever new dangers threatened, as happened nearly 80 years later, when the country seemed ready to break apart.

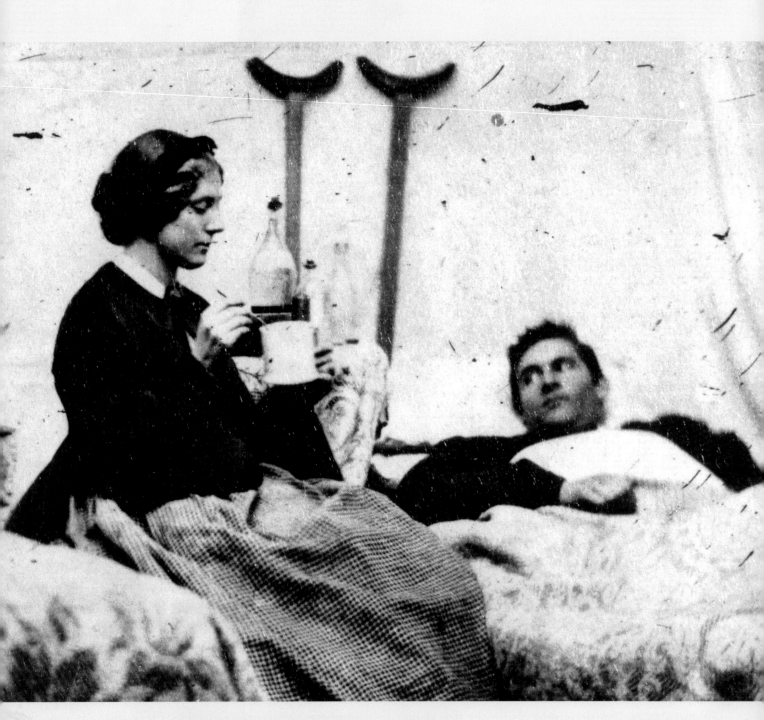

JUST BEFORE THE CIVIL WAR, CAMERAS WERE INVENTED. FOR THE
FIRST TIME PEOPLE COULD SEE PICTURES OF THE REAL MEN—AND
WOMEN—WHO SERVED IN WARTIME, LIKE THIS CIVIL WAR NURSE
WHO WAS CARING FOR AN INJURED SOLDIER.

CIVIL WAR

In 1861, when Elizabeth Wheeler's brother and other young men from her Massachusetts town headed off to fight at the start of the Civil War, she wanted to go, too. She noted that "had I been a man I should have counted [as] one of the number." But women still could not sign up as soldiers. "I did the next best thing, which was to offer my services in case the men should be sick or wounded." She became one of more than 10,000 women nurses in the Civil War. They were needed badly. More than half a million soldiers died in the Civil War, more than in any other war the U.S. has fought.

The war began in 1861 after 11 southern states broke away to form the Confederacy. They wanted individual states to have more power than the central government so each state could decide how to run things, especially whether to have slaves. President Abraham Lincoln and people in the North wanted to keep the country together and have a strong central government. Many also wanted to end slavery. Both sides believed so strongly in their cause that they went to war. Women of both the North and South took part as nurses, battlefield helpers, spies, and even soldiers-in-disguise.

More is known about what women did in this war than in the Revolution because many Civil War women wrote letters and books. Long before Louisa May Alcott wrote *Little Women,* she wrote a book called *Hospital Sketches* about being a Civil War nurse. She said nurses did "the hardest work of any part of the army except the mules." Women wrote more because more were educated. In the 30 years before the Civil War, more and more public schools started opening. Before then, most schools had been private and mainly for boys. Many of the new public schools let girls attend. A few women's colleges also had opened. Although middle-class women were still generally expected to stay home and care for the household, a small number of women had paying jobs, more in the North than in the South. They were mainly single women because it was not thought proper for married women to work. Some were teachers. A few were doctors. Some teenage girls worked in textile factories that had started opening in New England. So did low-income women, newly arrived from Ireland. However, women usually earned less than men and often were treated badly. Before the war, Clara Barton, who later started the American Red Cross, was the only female clerk in a government office. Some men in her office did not like her working there. They spat tobacco juice at her as she walked down the hall.

At the start of this war, many male doctors were not eager for women co-workers either. They wanted only men to be nurses. But hospitals filled up with so many wounded soldiers that there were not enough men to do the job. The Confederacy did not have an official medical system, but many Southern women volunteered on their own to nurse the wounded. In the North, Dorothea Dix offered to find women nurses for the Union Army. She was well known for having helped improve the care of mental patients in the U.S. The government made her the Superintendent of Women Nurses. It was a big step forward for a woman to have such an important position.

When the war started, Clara Barton was a government clerk in Washington, D.C. Earlier, she had taught school in Massachusetts. Some men she had taught were among the first to sign up as soldiers for the war. They took a train to Washington, where the Union Army was gathering. When they reached Washington, many were injured, having been attacked by Confederate supporters as the train passed through Maryland. Officials had no plans yet for what to do with injured soldiers. Clara Barton stepped in to help her former students. She brought some to a friend's house. The next morning she gathered up things in her apartment that a soldier might need and brought them to where the rest of the troops were.

That started her on a new career that earned her no pay but won her thanks from thousands of soldiers. She continued collecting supplies, not just for her former students. Soldiers' families and friends mailed her boxes of food, clothes, and other items. She stored the boxes in her room. When no more would fit, she rented a warehouse. Soon she wanted to make deliveries not only to soldiers in Washington but also to those on battlefields where the Union Army often ran out of supplies. It took a while to obtain permission, but before long she was loading boxes of supplies on wagons or trains heading for battle zones. After making a delivery, she stayed to treat the wounded. A doctor called her "the angel of the battlefield." She worked on her own or with friends to help the soldiers, whom she called "my boys." After the war, in 1881, Barton started the American Red Cross, which still helps people in need during war or during natural disasters.

NURSES EVERYWHERE

"All nurses are required to be plain looking women. Their dresses must be brown or black, with no bows, no curls, no jewelry, and no hoop-skirts." Those were Dorothea Dix's rules for the nurses she hired for the Union Army. She wanted serious-minded women who were at least 30 years old. Many were single. Others were married women who volunteered to be nurses after their husbands went off to war. Younger women nursed, too, either by pretending to be older or by volunteering with private nursing groups that let young women serve. Nurses with these private groups often worked for free. Dorothea Dix's nurses earned 40 cents a day, not much even back then. Southerner Sally Tompkins earned no salary but used her own money to set up a hospital for Confederate soldiers in a house in Richmond, Virginia.

At first, the North's nurses worked mainly at hospitals that were not too close to the fighting. Commanders did not want female nurses exposed to the dangers of a battlefield. However, some independent-minded women persuaded officials that women were tough enough to handle the danger. Annie Etheridge, a young woman in her early 20s, was one of the toughest. When her husband signed up with a Michigan regiment, she went along to help. She cooked and washed clothes, as did hundreds of other women, but mainly she took care of injured soldiers. One Union soldier wrote in his journal that in a battle in Virginia, he saw her "binding the wounds of a man when a shell exploded nearby, tearing him terribly, and removing a large portion of the skirt of her dress." She kept helping through all four years of the war.

Other Union nurses went to battlefields in trains, ships, or horse-drawn ambulances to pick up the wounded and bring them to hospitals. Hospitals were sometimes in hotels, schools, barns, or even tents. Several African-American

women were nurses on the Union Navy's first hospital ship, the *Red Rover.* Catholic nuns nursed on that ship, too.

None of the nurses for the North or South had much training. Although there were medical schools for doctors, there were no nursing schools yet. Some nurses for the Union Army took a few lessons from Dr. Elizabeth Blackwell, the first woman to graduate from a U.S. medical school. However, most nurses, male and female, learned on the job, watching doctors or other nurses.

Medical care was not very advanced. Doctors were just beginning to understand the importance of keeping things clean. Nurses would wash a soldier's wound and put on clean bandages. But if a wound became infected, there were no medicines to cure it. It would be about 80 years before the introduction of antibiotics, which can cure infections today. Back then, the main way to stop an infection from spreading was to amputate an infected

arm or leg. Frequently, cutting off an arm or a leg did not solve the problem, and infections killed many soldiers.

Besides infections, many soldiers had malaria, typhoid fever, and other diseases for which there were no good medicines. Twice as many soldiers died from these diseases as from battle wounds. Nurses became sick, too, and some died. Louisa May Alcott caught typhoid at an Army hospital in Washington, D.C. She went home to Massachusetts to recover and never returned to nursing.

Harriet Scott, a nurse from Vermont, wrote later about a visit President Lincoln made to the military hospital where she worked. The President said to her, "Well, nurse, we often hear the remark that these are days that try men's souls;—I think they try women's souls too. I shall remember you and all the noble women . . . when this land is at peace."

MEDAL OF HONOR

A few other women doctors helped with the war, too. Besides Dr. Blackwell, who did some training of nurses, there was also Dr. Mary Walker. She shocked people, not just because few women were doctors then, but also because she wore long pants called bloomers. She thought the long hoop skirts with tight waists that were considered stylish were bad for women. She felt women would be healthier in pants. Most people found this idea ridiculous. That didn't bother her.

When the war started, she asked the Union Army to hire her as a doctor. The Army refused, so she volunteered to work for free, first at a Washington hospital and then with Union forces in Virginia. Next she worked with troops in Tennessee. Male doctors there were not happy to have her, calling her a "medical monstrosity." That didn't stop her. Besides helping soldiers, she rode on horseback to treat families nearby.

On one ride, Confederate soldiers captured her. She spent four months in a Confederate prison. A prison official said he might free her if she dressed in female clothes. She refused, but was freed later in exchange for a Southern officer freed from a Union prison. Only then did the Army finally give her an official position with the title of Acting Assistant Surgeon. She was the first woman to have such a post.

After the war, she received the country's highest military award: the congressional Medal of Honor. In 1917, Congress said she should not have been given that medal. New rules said only people who had been in combat should have this medal. She was in her 80s and refused to give back her medal. In the 1970s, almost 60 years after her death, Congress decided it was all right for her to have the medal after all. By 2002, she was still the only woman to be awarded the Medal of Honor.

TAKING UP ARMS

A Union soldier injured in the chest at the Battle of Antietam in Virginia puzzled Clara Barton. This soldier did not want any help. She soon discovered that this soldier was a woman, one of hundreds of women from the North and the South who disguised themselves as male soldiers, just as Deborah Samson had done so many years before. These Civil War soldiers-in-disguise fought bravely. A few of these women even became officers.

A soldier's life had not changed much since the Revolutionary War, so it was still possible for a woman to get away with pretending to be a man. Sarah Emma Edmonds managed to join a Michigan regiment, saying her name was Franklin Thompson. The doctor who was supposed to examine her just shook her hand. However, once a woman was on duty, no matter how good her disguise, little things could cause her secret to be discovered. The proper table manners of an Iowa soldier made fellow soldiers realize that such a tidy eater had to be a woman. That ended her soldier days. The most common way that people discovered a "he" was a "she"

SUSIE KING TAYLOR

In 1862, at age 14, Susie King Taylor won her freedom from slavery when Union troops took over the part of Georgia where she lived. After the soldiers freed the slaves there, newly freed men joined an all-black company of Union soldiers. She signed up as their laundress.

"I gave my services willingly for four years and three months without receiving a dollar," she noted in a book she wrote after the war. She did more than wash clothes. This teen taught black soldiers to read.

Southern blacks were not allowed to learn to read, but a few did secretly. As a young slave girl, she had lived in the city of Savannah where there were some freed blacks. Her family made a daring plan. They arranged for her and her brother to go to the nearby home of a freed black to learn to read. She wrote that they walked there "every day about nine o'clock, with our books wrapped in paper to prevent the police or white persons from seeing them." If caught reading, they could be whipped. "The neighbors would see us going in sometimes, but they supposed we were there learning trades."

Besides teaching soldiers, she also cleaned and test-fired their rifles. She "could shoot straight and often hit the target." She also did some nursing. When an African-American regiment from Massachusetts fought on an island off the South Carolina coast, she took care of the wounded. So did Clara Barton. The two had met earlier while caring for black soldiers at an Army hospital in South Carolina. "Miss Barton was always very cordial toward me, and I honored her for her devotion and care for those men," noted Susie King Taylor. After the war, she started a school for Southern blacks and later moved to Massachusetts.

Altogether, about 180,000 African Americans served with Union forces.

happened when a soldier-in-disguise became so sick that a nurse or doctor had to examine her. That's probably why Sarah Emma Edmonds quit the Union Army after two years when she became very ill. She did not want to have a military doctor examine her and reveal her secret identity.

Some women warriors kept their secret all through the war. Jennie Hodgers called herself Albert Cashier and served with an Illinois regiment for three years. After the war, she kept dressing and living as a man for almost 50 years until 1911, when she was injured in an accident. Doctors finally discovered she was a woman. She was very old by then and had trouble learning how to walk in a long skirt without tripping. She told a reporter she joined the Union Army because the country needed soldiers and she wanted excitement. Women also became soldiers-in-disguise because they believed in their side's cause or because they did not want to be separated from husbands, brothers, or fathers who were in the military. Others disguised themselves as men because their families needed the money paid to new soldiers.

Near the war's end, the Confederacy needed soldiers so badly that some Southern women served in the Confederate Army without pretending to be men. Other Southern women, who also did not dress as men, formed all-female guard units that were not officially part of the Confederate Army. Most of the war's battles took place in the South, and these women wanted to be ready to defend their homes in case of an attack while their men were away fighting.

SPIES AND HOME-FRONT HELPERS

Some women were spies, including Harriet Tubman, the escaped slave who, before the war, traveled secretly into the South many times to lead other slaves to freedom. During the war she was a Union spy and nurse.

Female spies found unusual places to hide secret messages. Some hid papers and guns under their long, wide skirts. One Confederate spy, Rose O'Neal Greenhow, hid a message in the fancy hairdo of another female spy. Elizabeth Van Lew, a Union spy who lived in Richmond, Virginia, the Confederacy's capital, hid coded messages in hollowed-out eggs in a farm basket. She had gone to school up North, where she came to believe slavery was wrong. She had her family free their slaves and sent one of them, Mary Bowser, up North to go to school. Later, when war broke out, Elizabeth Van Lew organized a group of Northern supporters in Richmond to spy for the Union. In her spy group were former slaves including Mary Bowser, who pretended to be uneducated in order to work in the home of Jefferson Davis, the Confederacy's President. His family did not think she could read the papers on his desk, but she could. She passed the information along to Union supporters.

Besides spying, women on the home front took over jobs men had done before leaving to fight in the war. This time, in addition to running family farms, some women also took over jobs men had been doing in the clothing and shoe factories that had started opening in the years before the war, especially in the North. But after the war, when soldiers came home, they took back most of the jobs the women had been doing.

SARAH ROSETTA WAKEMAN

"I had to face the enemy bullets with my regiment. I was under fire about four hours," wrote Sarah Rosetta Wakeman in her last letter to her parents in New York. She was in Louisiana, fighting in the Union Army. It was in the spring of 1864, almost two years after she disguised herself at age 19 as a young man in order to join a New York regiment.

Her main reason for joining was to earn pay to send her parents, who were poor farmers. She also liked being independent. She wrote her parents many letters, telling them in one that "I am well and enjoy myself first rate." She bragged of handling a gun "as well as the rest of them." She wrote, "I will Dress as I am a mind to . . . and if they don't let me Alone they will be sorry for it." She planned to buy a farm after the war.

In early 1864, her regiment sailed to New Orleans to begin a 400-mile march through hot, steamy forests to try to reach Texas. Her regiment came under attack and had to retreat. She had written her parents that "I don't believe there are any Rebel's bullet made for me." What harmed her was not an enemy bullet, but the dirty water she and other soldiers were given to drink on the long march. The military did not yet have good ways to provide fresh, clean water and food for troops. She and hundreds of others became ill with dysentery (severe diarrhea). Back then, doctors could do little for this. She died and was buried in New Orleans. If doctors discovered she was female, they did not tell. On her grave marker is the male name she used in the Army: Lyons Wakeman.

UNITED ONCE AGAIN

The war ended in April 1865, when Confederate troops surrendered. The country was united again. Slavery was abolished, and within a few years newly freed African-American men had the right to vote. However, women still could not vote, no matter what their race. Many women who had served in the war thought it was time to change that, so they became active in the Woman's Suffrage Movement. This effort to gain women the right to vote had started before the war but picked up steam afterward. It would be more than 50 years before their efforts succeeded. Dr. Mary Walker started a campaign to persuade the government to pay Civil War nurses pensions, like those paid to soldiers. In the 1890s, the government finally did this, but wound up providing pensions to only a small portion of the nurses.

The Civil War led to some new opportunities for women. Before the war, doctors had not paid much attention to nurses, male or female. The excellent job nurses did in wartime made doctors realize how much patients could be helped by good nursing care. So in the 1870s, less than 10 years after the war, nursing schools opened for the first time in the U.S. Nursing soon became a mostly female profession, joining teaching as one of the few professions considered suitable for women. Despite that, the armed forces took a step backward and, for the next 30 years, went back to having only male nurses. Officials were still not ready to let women be a permanent part of the armed forces. That would change toward the end of the century when the nation found itself once again at war.

THE START OF SOMETHING NEW

A new war—the Spanish-American War—started in April 1898. It was fought partly to protect Americans doing business in Cuba and partly to help Cuba win its independence from Spain. Fighting occurred in places that were under Spanish control: on the Caribbean islands of Cuba and Puerto Rico as well as on the Philippine Islands in the South Pacific. U.S. forces easily defeated Spain after about four months. But the fight against disease went less well. Many more soldiers died from tropical diseases, such as malaria, typhoid, and yellow fever, than were killed in the fighting. Once again the military counted on women to help.

In an effort to make the military more professional, the Army no longer allowed female battlefield cooks and laundresses. There were also no reports of women disguised as soldiers. By then, Army doctors examined new soldiers carefully, using a card with a diagram of a body

on it. Doctors noted on this Figure Card any scars or marks a soldier had on his body. This helped officials catch men who quit the Army as a result of getting in trouble and then tried to sign up again using a new name so they could still earn a soldier's pay. Once doctors began using the Figure Card, a woman would have a hard time sneaking in as a man.

But about 1,500 women, including about 80 African Americans and several Native Americans, did serve in this war as nurses. Almost all had graduated from the new nursing schools. Some served in military hospitals in the U.S. Others served outside the U.S., working at hospitals on the islands of Cuba or Puerto Rico. Serving overseas was new for military women. The military hospitals on those islands were often in tents, and the nurses often slept in tents, too. Some nurses also served on board hospital ships that picked

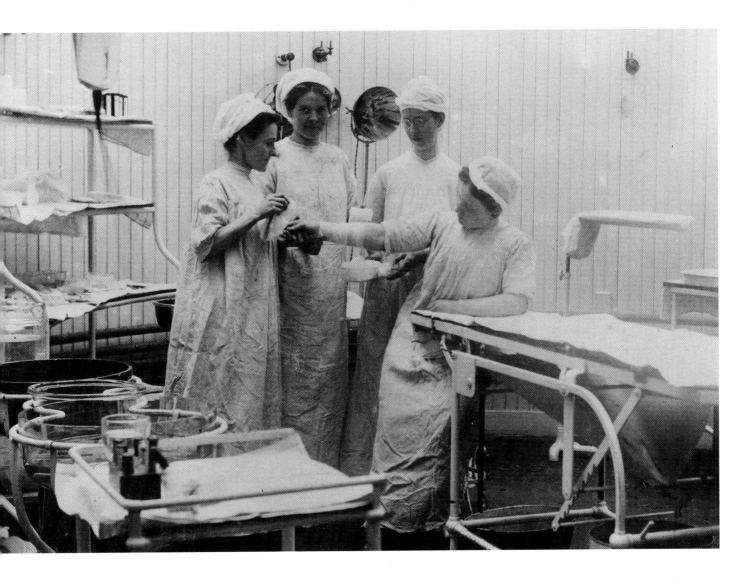

up wounded soldiers and brought them back to the U.S. None of the nurses was officially part of the Army. They were civilians, working for the Army. The Army paid them a salary—$30 to $50 a month—and after the war, gave them pensions. Women did not have to mount a huge campaign to receive them, as happened after the Civil War.

The nurses did such a good job that the Army made a big change. In 1901, the Army created its first official female unit: the Army Nurse Corps. The Navy followed in 1908, starting the Navy Nurse Corps. From then on, women nurses no longer would be hired only as temporary civilian helpers during emergencies. They would be part of the military. However, these servicewomen were not treated the same as servicemen. For many years, Army and Navy nurses could not have military titles, such as lieutenant. Even so, these new nursing corps marked a big step forward in the long, slow process of changing the military from being only for men.

THESE NURSES ARE WORKING IN AN ARMY HOSPITAL IN CUBA DURING THE SPANISH-AMERICAN WAR. "WE WERE CARING FOR BOYS WHO HAD GONE INTO THE SERVICE TO FIGHT BUT WERE STRICKEN WITH DISEASE," SAID ROSE HEAVREN (SECOND FROM THE RIGHT). "THEY WERE SUCH A FINE LOT OF BOYS THAT IT WAS VERY SAD TO THINK WE COULD DO SO LITTLE FOR THEM." THERE STILL WERE NO GOOD MEDICINES TO CURE THE TROPICAL DISEASES SOLDIERS CAUGHT DURING THIS WAR.

SOME OF THE NAVY'S FEMALE YEOMEN
WHO SERVED IN CALIFORNIA

WORLD WAR I

1917 - 1918

"I'm a regular sailor, as much so as any man in the service," Loretta Walsh proudly proclaimed in a newspaper article in the spring of 1917. This 20-year-old from Pennsylvania made headlines for doing something no woman had done before. She was the first woman to be a full, official member of the U.S. Navy. She signed up with the Navy on March 21, 1917, a few weeks before the U.S. entered World War I. Women had been working for the Navy as nurses since 1908, but they were not full members and did not have military titles. But Loretta Walsh had an official Navy title—yeoman. She did the same work and earned the same pay as a male yeoman. So did the Navy's nearly 12,000 other female yeomen who served in World War I.

A yeoman is a member of the Navy who does office work. Until the late 1800s, office work was mainly for men, both in and out of the military. That changed with the invention of the typewriter. Companies began hiring women as typists. Women performed so well that by 1910 they made up more than half of the office workers in the U.S. business world. It was beginning to be considered all right for young women to do office work for a few years before marrying and raising a family. However, most American women still did not have paying jobs. Fewer than one-quarter were employed. These were mainly single women, because people still thought marriage and a job did not mix. Only one out of every ten married women had a paying job; these women were often from poor families, and they frequently worked as household servants.

Many of the country's female office workers came to the aid of the Navy in early 1917 when it found itself in a jam. War had started a few years before in Europe, where Germany and its allies were fighting against Great Britain, France, and Russia. The U.S. tried to stay out of this war. But when German submarines sank several U.S. ships that were sailing to Britain, the U.S. believed it had to go to war. So, in April 1917, America joined in the fight against Germany to make the world "safe for democracy," as President Woodrow Wilson said. But the U.S. did not have enough troops.

The head of the Navy, Josephus Daniels, had realized this in early 1917. If the country went to war, he knew he would soon need a lot more sailors, not only to serve on ships, but to do office jobs at headquarters. Unlike many men then, he supported women's rights. He figured if women took over much of the office work, more men would be available to serve on ships. The easiest way to round up thousands of women in a hurry would be to sign them up in the Naval Reserves, like male sailors. He asked, "Is there any regulation which specifies that a Navy yeoman be a man?" There wasn't. So the Navy began signing up women, starting with Loretta Walsh.

"What'll I say to my grandchildren . . . when they ask me: 'What did you do in the Great War, Grandma?'" That was part of a magazine article Sergeant Martha Wilchinski wrote during the war. She could tell her grandkids she worked in the Marine publicity office, writing humorous articles for Marine magazines and having publicity photos taken of her, such as this one, to encourage other people to enlist. She had studied to be a writer at college.

There wasn't much that was funny about war, but her articles made people chuckle. In one, she wrote about one problem of having women in the military: Who should enter a very small elevator first—a female Marine or a male officer? "If I am a lady and he's a gentleman, I go in first," she wrote, according to what was considered polite behavior back then. But if he was higher in rank, he should go first. She told what happened when she was in that situation. "I thought I'd wait and see what he'd do. . . . he stepped forward and I stepped back. Then he stepped back and I stepped forward. Then we both stepped back. I was getting pretty dizzy by that time. I guess he was too. Then we both squeezed in at the same time. I guess that's what they mean by military tactics."

FREE A MAN TO FIGHT

A year later, in 1918, the Marines started signing up women office workers, too. Marine women started as privates, like new male recruits, and earned the same pay as men. If women did well, they could be promoted to become corporals or sergeants. The Marines used a slogan to encourage women to sign up: "Free a Man to Fight." Thousands of women rushed to join. Before being accepted by either the Marines or the Navy, women had to have a medical checkup and often took a typing test, too. They were supposed to be at least 18 and single. Only 305 made it into the Marines because the war ended three months after the Marines started recruiting women.

Many Navy and Marine women were high school graduates, and some had even been to college. Although most boys and girls at that time attended primary schools, fewer than a third went to high school. There, girls were taking the lead; many more than half the high school students then were girls. However, few girls went to college, where males still greatly outnumbered females.

Newspapers printed letters from people who did not want women in the military. One suggested women could do more by staying home and "raising a family of boys." Cute nicknames sprang up: Yeomanette or Marinette. Officials did not like that. "These women are as much a

part of the Navy as the men," said an admiral. "They are yeomen." However, after a woman was sent by mistake to work on a ship (where women were not allowed), the Navy added an "F" for "female" to their titles. After that, they were called "Yeomen (F)." When officials looked down a list of yeomen's names, the (F) showed which ones should not have ship duty. The Marine Corps said its women were in the "Marine Reserves (F)."

Although women took over much of the office work, men still worked in military offices, too. At first, some men were not thrilled to have female co-workers. Officials feared that a woman could not do as much work as a man. But the women did more than their fair share. A few served in Europe, but most worked at Navy or Marine headquarters in Washington, D.C., or at military offices around the country. Most were secretaries, clerks, messengers, or telephone operators. A few received specialized training and did jobs that were not thought of as "women's work," such as helping make ammunition. "Excellent," was how the head of the Marine Corps rated the women's work. The head of the Navy agreed. Marine Private First Class Edith Macias said most men "did not look down or frown upon us" but were "glad to have us. We were given a job to do and we did it."

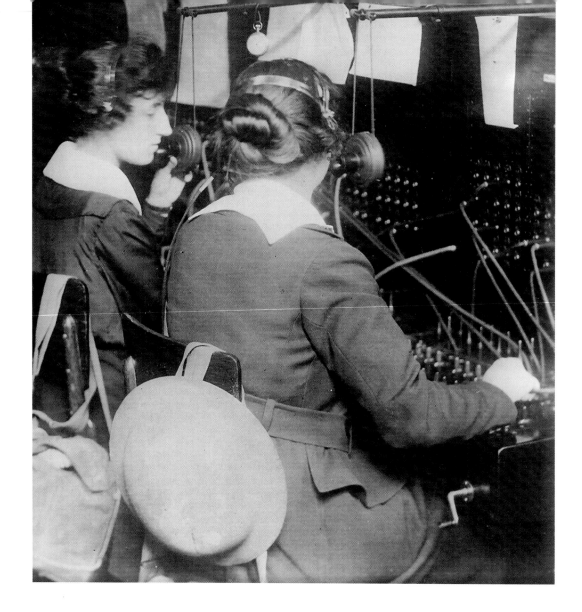

GRACE BANKER PADDOCK (RIGHT, HERE) AND ANOTHER "HELLO GIRL" ARE RUNNING A SWITCHBOARD AT AN ARMY OFFICE IN FRANCE. THEY HAVE HELMETS ON THEIR CHAIRS TO PUT ON IN CASE THEY COME UNDER ATTACK.

SWITCHBOARD SOLDIERS

Army generals wanted to sign up female office workers, too. However, Army rules said only "male persons" could join the Army Reserves. To change the rules, Congress would have to pass a new law, something it would not do. General John Pershing, commander of U.S. forces in Europe, found a way around these rules because he had a telephone crisis. Back then, phone calls did not go through automatically. An operator had to connect you. Almost all telephone operators in the business world were female. But French women operators at General Pershing's headquarters in France were having trouble, mainly because they spoke little English. He asked the Army to send American women to run his phones. More than 7,000 women applied. About 200 were selected to serve overseas. They were hired as civilians and were not officially part of the military. Soldiers nicknamed them "Hello Girls." General Pershing called them "switchboard soldiers."

His headquarters was far from the Front, where the battles were fought. So were most of the other Army offices where Hello Girls worked. One of the women taught soldiers how to run portable switchboards to use during battle. However, a few women served at the Front in the last months of the war. Grace Banker Paddock and several others ran portable switchboards that were set up a few miles from the fighting in northeastern France. They moved with the troops, sometimes sleeping in a barn or in old sheds—"flimsy affairs set down in a sea of mud," she recalled later. Black cloth covered the windows at night so light would not leak out to "announce our presence to the raiding German planes." During a battle, she had only "two or three hours of rest" because she had to keep phone lines open so officers could send emergency orders to the troops. "Everybody worked hard, yet no one seemed to complain. The excitement carried us along."

"AS BRAVE AS MEN"

"One need never tell me that women can't do as much, stand as much, and be as brave as men," wrote Julia Stimson in a letter to her family in the fall of 1917. As an Army nurse in France, she had a chance to observe many brave American women in action. In her letter, she described the conditions faced by nurses serving near battle zones, with "whistling, banging shells exploding around them." About 21,000 U.S. women were military nurses during this war. Nearly half served in Europe, where the fighting took place. The rest worked in military hospitals in the U.S.

This time, the military did not have to worry about where to find nurses. The newly created Army and Navy Nurse Corps had a few hundred female nurses on duty when the war started. About 8,000 other nurses had signed up through the Red Cross to be in the Reserves, promising to serve if there was a war. When the U.S. declared war, they reported for duty. Soon thousands more signed up. All had graduated from nursing school. Many of them had also gone to college.

Some nurses traveled with the troops, packing up and moving medical tents from battle to battle. Wounded soldiers were brought first to these frontline hospitals. There were so many wounded soldiers that they often had to lie on the ground because frontline units did not have enough beds. Soldiers who needed treatment right away were cared for there. Others went by motorized ambulance to base hospitals farther from the fighting. Most nurses worked at base hospitals. Julia Stimson was chief nurse at a base hospital that was a series of tents set up on an old racetrack.

"I cried all that first day," wrote Laura Frost Smith in a letter home from her frontline unit in France. This Army nurse was put right to work caring for seriously injured soldiers. "I thought they had made a mistake by putting us through that experience so soon, but maybe it was for the good and I could stand anything after that miserable week."

It was not just the work that was hard. At the Front, nurses usually lived in tents. Much of the time it was cold and rainy, which made the dirt around the tents turn into thick, slippery mud. Often, there were no bathtubs. Nurses took sponge baths, using a pot of water heated on a small stove. Things were not much better at base hospitals, which often had no bathtubs either.

LILLIANN BLACKWELL DIAL

"I am an impatient creature, always eager for experiences," wrote Lilliann Blackwell Dial in her diary. Her search for adventure led this North Dakota woman to be an Army nurse in France. For someone who rode in horse-drawn carriages as a girl, she had plenty of new experiences there, watching battles fought with that new invention, the airplane. She worked with a mobile hospital unit that traveled with the troops, never staying in one place more than a week or so. The work was tough, caring for thousands of injured men without enough helpers or supplies. She handled even the toughest challenges with enthusiasm. But one morning, she lost her cool.

Her unit had to pack up suddenly and move again. The soldier who was to help her had a high fever. The stove did not work. There was too little food. "Things were in wild disorder," she noted, with "clothing strewn everywhere, utensils under the beds, no dressings, no linen, no water." Then, in walked the commanding officer. "We were 'bawled out for fair' in regulation, military style!" That did it. As he walked away, she followed and let him know why things were a mess. A few minutes later, he sent food, a new stove, and another soldier to help. "The tears kept coming all day but no one seemed to mind," she wrote in her diary. "I guess it pays to go to Headquarters with complaints." The next day, she was back to normal.

A NEW GROUP OF AMERICAN NURSES ARRIVES TO WORK AT AN ARMY HOSPITAL BEING BUILT IN FRANCE IN 1918. THERE WERE SO MANY INJURED SOLDIERS TO CARE FOR THAT NURSES AT THESE UNITS WERE ALWAYS DELIGHTED TO WELCOME MUCH NEEDED EXTRA HELPERS.

HELEN FAIRCHILD

"I may have some exciting tales to tell you," wrote Helen Fairchild in a letter to her family before sailing to France in 1917 with the first group of Army nurses. She worked first at a base hospital on the French coast. She wrote home about beautiful sunsets and how much she hated wearing a nurse's uniform all the time. "Just as soon as I get home I am going to get dresses [of] all colors of the rainbow," she noted. Soon she volunteered to work with a medical unit closer to the fighting. She wrote about how hard it was to keep her white uniform clean "in a place where it rains …every day, and we all live in tents, and wade through mud to and from the operating room."

She didn't write home about bombs falling nearby, probably so she wouldn't worry her family. Nor did she write about the mustard gas that burned the soldiers she treated. The gas stayed in a soldier's clothing. This meant that a nurse could breathe it in when cleaning a patient's sores. Soon she became ill. She had suffered from stomach problems in the past. Experts now feel the gas she breathed in may have made that condition worse. Medical care back then was not advanced enough to cure her. In January 1918, she died. The Army gave her a military funeral and buried her in France, where she had been an Army nurse for just six months.

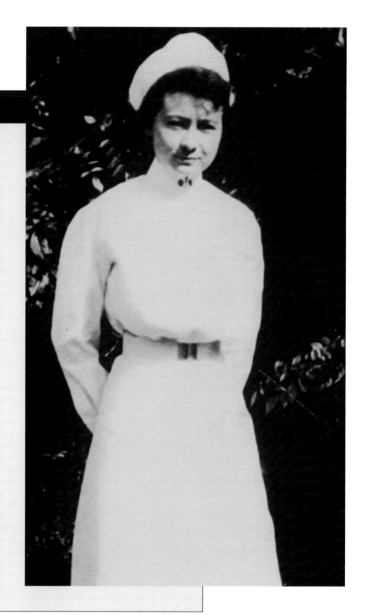

NEW DANGERS – NEW CHANCES

Nurses in this war had to treat new kinds of injuries caused by a terrible new form of warfare: poison gas attacks. Both sides used tear gas and other dangerous gases, but the worst was the mustard gas used by the Germans. It burned skin and damaged eyes and lungs. In general, soldiers received better care than in earlier wars because the medical service was better organized, and doctors and nurses were more skilled. But antibiotics still had not been introduced, so infected wounds continued to be a danger. A few diseases that had caused much suffering in earlier wars were less of a problem. For example, vaccinations protected people against typhoid. This was the first war that U.S. forces had fought where disease was not the main cause of death for soldiers.

Sadly, disease *was* the main cause of death for U.S. servicewomen. More than 400 nurses as well as 57 Navy Yeomen (F) died, mostly from a deadly flu that appeared suddenly near the end of the war. It was especially bad in the U.S., where hospitals were so filled with flu patients that there were not enough nurses to care for everyone. This made the military finally give African-American nurses a chance.

About 1,800 African-American nursing school graduates had signed up with the Red Cross to be military nurses. However, they were not allowed to be part of the military during the war, although Native-

American nurses were allowed to serve. The U.S. was still a very segregated country. So was its military. For example, the more than 350,000 black soldiers had to serve in all-black units, where they often faced other forms of discrimination.

Attitudes changed when the flu crisis became so bad that officials realized they needed all the help they could get. In the fall of 1918, Army officials asked Aileen Cole Stewart and a few other black nurses to go to West Virginia to care for sick coal miners. She and the others would still not be Army nurses. Instead they would work as civilians. She agreed to go to West Virginia because, as she wrote later, a miner "was as important in his way as a soldier." The military needed coal to fuel its ships.

A month after she started caring for the miners, the war ended. Two days after the fighting stopped, the Army finally asked her to join the Army Nurse Corps. She and 17 other black women then became the first African Americans allowed to be in the Army Nurse Corps. They worked at Army bases in Ohio and Illinois. Although these new Army nurses had to live in segregated housing, she said, "We were liked, accepted, and respected by officers and men."

Fourteen African-American women also performed well as Yeomen (F), working during the war at a Navy office in Washington, D.C.

AILEEN COLE STEWART (FAR LEFT, FRONT ROW) WITH OTHER AFRICAN-AMERICAN NURSES WHO FINALLY BECAME ARMY NURSES RIGHT AFTER WORLD WAR I ENDED. THEY WERE NOT ALLOWED TO JOIN THE ARMY NURSE CORPS DURING THE WAR.

ADDIE HUNTON

"We deliberately planned to make our chocolate so good that they would really come for it." That's what Addie Hunton and a co-worker wrote in a book about working in YMCA canteens in France during the war. Tasty snacks weren't the only reasons her canteen was a hit. She was one of three African-American women who were allowed overseas to work in canteens during the war. Their canteens were for black soldiers, who were often not permitted in other canteens. As her book noted, she felt it was sad that "prejudice could follow us for three thousand miles across the Atlantic." Prejudice at home made it hard for her even to gain permission to go to France. When she finally arrived, black soldiers were overjoyed. She and the two other women became "mothers, sisters and friends to thousands of men."

She was in her 50s, a college graduate and former teacher. She enjoyed taking care of young, homesick soldiers. Over cups of hot chocolate, she had them talk about home. She offered books, games, movies, and help with reading and writing. She even found musical instruments for a band. She stayed on after the war, until the troops went home. By then 16 other black women had been allowed to work in the canteens. The discrimination she saw in the war led her to work later with groups to promote better understanding among the races.

OTHER WAYS OF SERVING

Women doctors were another group that was not allowed to serve in the U.S. military during World War I. Quite a few women had been trained as doctors by then, but many people still thought being a doctor was a "man's job." However, a few women doctors worked at Army hospitals as civilians. Others went to France on their own to work at clinics run by a women's group or at hospitals for the French Army.

More than 5,000 other U.S. women went to Europe to volunteer with private groups, such as the Red Cross, Salvation Army, and YMCA (Young Men's Christian Association). They visited hospitals to bring supplies.

Others ran canteens where troops could relax during time off, play games, have a snack, or listen to singers. Some canteens were set up in trucks that traveled with the troops. Back home, thousands of other women once again took over jobs men left behind when they went off to war. The women did things few people at that time thought women could handle, such as working in steel mills or running elevators and streetcars. As in earlier wars, women generally had to turn these jobs back to men when the troops came home. The percentage of women working during peacetime would not rise greatly until much later in the century.

FULL CITIZENS AT LAST

After the war ended with Germany's surrender in November 1918, hundreds of U.S. women received military awards to honor their service to the country. Julia Stimson, Grace Banker Paddock, and more than 20 others earned the Distinguished Service Medal, the highest honor for people not in combat. However, four Army nurses who came under enemy attack received an award usually given only to those involved in combat: the Distinguished Service Cross.

Most servicewomen also received military pensions. But African-American nurses received nothing. The Army said pensions were only for those who served during the fighting; African-American nurses were allowed in the Army Nurse Corps only after fighting stopped. Hello Girls and 2,000 physical therapy aides also received no benefits because they were hired as civilians and were never actually in the Army. Almost 60 years later, in 1977, Congress passed a law that said that these two groups had done real military work and should have received benefits. By that time, few of them were alive to enjoy the honor.

There was one special honor that went to all women of all races. It was a direct result of the remarkable contributions made by the 34,000 military women and the thousands of civilian women who helped in this war. This honor came in 1920 when the 19th Amendment to the Constitution was ratified. It said that a woman could no longer be denied the right to vote. As President Wilson said, if women could not vote, "we shall have fought to safeguard a democracy which . . . we have never bothered to create."

After the war, a few hundred nurses stayed in the Army and Navy nursing corps. For about the next 20 years, nurses would be the only women allowed in the military. All others were discharged. This first experiment in having women office workers as part of the military had come to an end.

People at the time thought something else had also come to an end: warfare. Many believed in the slogan of the day, that this was the "war to end all wars." Sadly, just over 20 years later, war threatened again, and once more women would be counted on to help.

AVIATION MACHINIST'S
MATE VIOLET FALKUM WAS
ONE OF 25,000 NAVY
WOMEN WHO WERE
TRAINED TO PERFORM
IMPORTANT ROLES IN
MILITARY AVIATION
DURING WORLD WAR II.
HERE, SHE TURNS THE
PROPELLER ON A NAVY
PLANE AT A NAVAL AIR
STATION IN FLORIDA.

WORLD WAR II

1941 - 1945

"Girls, get into your uniforms, this is the real thing!" That is the urgent message a Navy nurse heard when she answered the phone on Sunday morning, December 7, 1941. She was having breakfast with other nurses, after working late the night before at Pearl Harbor Naval Hospital in Hawaii. That phone call ended her plans for a quiet day off. Japanese planes were bombing American ships and airfields in Pearl Harbor. She put on her uniform and raced to the hospital, as the first injured sailors arrived. The attack surprised not only nurses but also the whole country and caused the U.S. to enter World War II. War had been raging for more than two years in Europe and Asia, as Nazi Germany and its ally, Japan, attacked many countries. The U.S. had tried to stay out of the war. But after this surprise attack killed more than 2,300 Americans, the U.S. had to defend itself.

Women in the Army and Navy Nurse Corps were there right from the start. But nurses were the only U.S. women on military duty at that time. No others had been allowed to serve since World War I. That soon changed, thanks to Congresswoman Edith Nourse Rogers. She had seen military women in action during World War I when she was a YMCA and Red Cross volunteer. In early 1941, months before the Pearl Harbor attack, she realized the U.S. might soon go to war again. She knew the country would need women's help. She introduced a bill in Congress to create a women's branch of the Army. Her plan was not popular. Many people still felt a woman's place was in the home. Only about one out of every four women had a paying job, and these working gals were mainly single. Some married women had jobs, but the majority did not.

Pearl Harbor changed many minds. The military was not ready. Millions more troops were needed. This new war was much bigger than any earlier one. Battles had to be fought around the globe: in Europe, Africa, Asia, and the islands of the South Pacific. The military needed all the help it could get. So in May 1942, Congress passed Congresswoman Rogers's bill, creating a women's corps for the Army. Chosen to head the new corps was Oveta Culp Hobby, college graduate, newspaper publisher, wife of a former Texas governor, and mom to two kids.

A few months later, the other branches of the armed forces had new women's units, too. About 350,000 women served in these units, as well as in the Army and Navy Nurse Corps—ten times as many as in World War I. Many were right out of high school; others were college graduates. Most were single, in their 20s and 30s, but some were older and married. The good job they did led, after the war, to women finally becoming permanent members of the armed forces.

Corporal Irene Brion (second from the left) and a small group of WACs spent a year on islands in the South Pacific "waging war against the Japanese by pushing pencils in our offices," as she noted in her memoirs. Her job was to help figure out a number code that Japan used in its secret messages. She had learned some Japanese as well as how to crack codes during training at a base in Virginia. Then she and 18 other Army decoders were shipped off to the South Pacific island of New Guinea. Army telephone operators stationed around the Pacific would try to hear Japanese messages, which were made up of numbers. These operators wrote down the numbers and sent them to the decoders. Her group worked on codes that told what was in Japanese ships. Part of the code was already known. Each new word she figured out helped create a code dictionary that other decoders could use to read other messages.

It was hot in New Guinea and in the Philippines where she worked later. But she said, "I loved the work. I would lose all track of time pursuing the meaning of the messages." She felt proud because "this job hadn't been done by women before." After the war, she went back to what she had done before: teaching sixth grade in New York. Later she moved to California, but kept on teaching.

MORE THAN TYPING AND TELEPHONES

The Navy had a clever name for its female unit: WAVES, which stood for "Women Accepted for Volunteer Emergency Service." Coast Guard women were called SPARs, from the Coast Guard motto "Semper Paratus" ("always prepared"). The Marine Corps had a no-nonsense name for its females: Marines. At first, Army women were called WAACs, for Women's Army Auxiliary Corps. Soon the Army dropped the "A" for "auxiliary," and Army females became simply WACs. They had military titles and the same pay as men, just like the WAVES, SPARs, and female Marines. Even nurses were finally allowed to have military titles. However, none of the women could rise all the way up in rank. In the WACs there could only be one full colonel, the head of the WACs. Other WACs could be promoted only as far as lieutenant colonel, which is a step below full colonel. WACs served in the U.S. and in every part of the world where U.S. forces fought. So did Army and Navy nurses. However, for most of the war, WAVES, SPARs, and female Marines were allowed to work only on the U.S. mainland.

As in World War I, women would do noncombat jobs so men could go fight. However, World War II women tackled more kinds of noncombat jobs. Some drove and repaired trucks and jeeps. Others were radar specialists, metalworkers, radio operators, and code experts. It was unusual for women to do such technical jobs. Before World War II, women with paying jobs did mainly "women's jobs": salesclerk, nurse, teacher, social worker, librarian, housekeeper, or office worker. But because the military did not have enough men, it trained women for its technical jobs. Many jobs were in the new field of flying. Almost half the Army women were called Air WACs because they worked for the Army Air Forces. WAVES and female Marines also worked in aviation. (There was not yet a separate branch called the Air Force.) These women ran airport control towers, packed parachutes, repaired planes, and taught navigation skills to male pilots. A few WAVES were crew members on noncombat flights.

No WAVES, Air WACs or female Marines served as pilots. However there were 1,102 female pilots who flew for the Army Air Forces. They were in a separate unit called the WASPs (Women Airforce Service Pilots). They were hired as civilians and so were not in the military, but they flew thousands of noncombat military missions in the U.S. Some delivered new planes to bases so the planes could go overseas into combat. Others test-flew repaired planes. Some piloted planes that pulled cloth targets through the sky so new soldiers on the ground could practice hitting the targets with ammunition from antiaircraft guns.

THESE WASPS PILOTED THE B-17 BOMBER SHOWN HERE, NAMED "PISTOL PACKIN' MAMA" IN THEIR HONOR. WASPS FLEW EVERY KIND OF PLANE THE ARMY AIR FORCES HAD.

BOOT CAMP

Before most servicewomen started work, they had to go through basic training, or "boot camp" as it is called in the Navy and Marines. They spent several weeks doing tough physical exercise and learning to march, obey military rules, and be part of a disciplined team. It was similar to the training men received, just without the weapons training. However, men and women trained separately.

Part of learning teamwork involved living in a room with a group of women and keeping that room spotless so it could pass inspections. If one person messed up, the whole unit suffered. "The inspectors might check into anything; might even brush their white-gloved fingers along surfaces to see if they had been dusted," noted WAVE Lieutenant Helen Clifford Gunter. The women also had to learn military lingo. A dining room was called the "mess," rumors were "scuttlebutt," and a Navy bathroom was a "head." The military also came up with a way to address its new female officers: Instead of "Yes, Sir," troops were to say, "Yes, Ma'am."

ARMY NURSES, DURING BASIC TRAINING IN THE U.S. BEFORE BEING SHIPPED OVERSEAS, LEARN HOW TO CRAWL ALONG THE GROUND TO AVOID BEING HIT BY LIVE AMMUNITION EXPLODING OVERHEAD.

THIS NAVY FLIGHT NURSE, ENSIGN JANE KENDEIGH, WAS FIRED ON, BUT NOT INJURED, AS SHE HELPED AIRLIFT WOUNDED TROOPS TO SAFETY DURING FIGHTING ON THE PACIFIC ISLAND OF IWO JIMA.

UNDER ATTACK

Servicewomen were not supposed to be in combat, but many served so close to the fighting that they came under attack. The ship carrying some of the first Army women overseas in late 1942 was torpedoed by a German submarine. A British warship rescued these five women officers from a lifeboat bobbing in the sea and took them to North Africa so they could begin working at U.S. Army headquarters there. American forces were trying to drive German troops out of Africa. These women officers made preparations for other women who would arrive a few weeks later to drive trucks, run the phone system, and do other clerical work. Army nurses were already there, caring for wounded soldiers. The next year, when U.S. forces moved on to fight in Sicily and Italy, the nurses and WACs went, too, working in rugged conditions, often near the fighting. WACs continued to do whatever support work was needed, from being translators to putting secret messages into code. There was great danger working so close to the fighting. Six Army nurses died in early 1944 when a bomb hit hospital tents during a battle on Italy's Anzio beach.

In the summer of 1944, when U.S. forces landed on French beaches in the D-Day invasion, nurses and WACs were there as well. They traveled with the troops as they battled to victory across France and Germany.

A new kind of nurse was in this war: flight nurses, who served with both the Army and the Navy. They worked on planes that airlifted the wounded to hospitals. These nurses faced danger not only from enemy fire but also from plane crashes. Aircraft often had to fly in bad weather in order to complete urgent rescue missions.

Nurses also served on hospital ships, but not on combat ships. As U.S. forces battled on island after island in the South Pacific, hospital ships picked up the wounded to give them treatment and bring them to hospitals in safe places like New Zealand or on islands freed from enemy control. Ships sailed a zigzag course to make it harder for submarines to find them and attack. But submarines weren't the only danger. Six Army nurses died in 1945 when a Japanese plane crashed into their hospital ship in a suicide attack. Altogether, more than 400 U.S. servicewomen and nurses died serving in World War II.

MUD AND MOSQUITOES

"It was like camping out at scout camp, only muddier and colder," said First Lieutenant Dorothy Steinbis Davis. She was explaining what it was like living in a tent as an Army nurse at a frontline hospital. She coped with many of the same hardships that World War I nurses had. It was just as rough for WACs who traveled with the troops. But at least these World War II women did not have to shiver in dresses like World War I nurses had. By the 1940s, it was finally all right for women to wear pants. "We wore wool Army pants like the soldiers," said First Lieutenant Davis. "We had combat jackets and combat boots." They also used helmets to protect them from bombs and to hold water for taking sponge baths and washing clothes.

On islands in the South Pacific, nurses and WACs also wore long pants and long-sleeved shirts. They did this not to keep warm, but as protection against mosquitoes that carried tropical diseases. It was so hot on these tropical islands that "by noon the back of my shirt would be drenched," recalled WAC Corporal Irene Brion. She and others in the Army also had to cope with the uncomfortable cots they slept on in their tents. A World War II Army cot had no mattress, just a thin piece of canvas. To make it more comfy, she slept on top of one of her blankets. Sometimes she folded her pants, put them under the blanket, and slept on them, too, in order to press out wrinkles. Draped around her cot was a huge net to keep out mosquitoes. There were also other pests on those islands: tarantulas, scorpions, and black widow spiders. A 12-foot-long lizard with a big swishing tail raced under hospital tents that had been set up on stilts in the middle of a jungle where First Lieutenant Sally Hitchcock Pullman worked on the Philippine island of Leyte. It didn't hurt anyone but made its way back to a nearby swamp.

During less busy periods, there was some time to relax, read books, or watch movies shown at the base where they lived. First Lieutenant Pullman liked to go walking on the beach. But on one outing, she and her friends had to dive for cover as an enemy plane "sprayed the beach with his guns," she wrote in a letter home. But she assured her parents that "I wanted to serve and I'm doing it. We...are really helping so many." The help they gave was good, thanks to more advanced medical treatments. There were new medicines for tropical diseases and a few new wonder drugs—including the antibiotic penicillin—that could finally treat infections. Most soldiers survived if they made it to military hospitals. Sadly, many died before getting there. Almost half a million Americans lost their lives in this war.

THESE ARMY NURSES ARE USING HELMETS AS WASH BASINS AT THEIR CAMP IN OKINAWA, AN ISLAND NEAR JAPAN.

NOT FAIR

In 1943, there were rumors both within the military and in the newspapers that servicewomen were misbehaving. The rumors were not true. Rumors also said the women had signed up only to find boyfriends. That bothered Lieutenant Gunter, who said, "I had joined primarily to help win the war, but also to participate in . . . the greatest adventure of my generation." The head of the Marines issued an order that treating Marine women "with disrespect" would "not be tolerated." As military men saw what a great job women did, attitudes began to change, and soon the rumors stopped.

However, some unfair conditions continued. The two nursing corps were in a confusing situation. Although nurses had titles and uniforms and had to obey military rules, they were not full members of the force. Sometimes they earned less than others with the same rank. Female doctors had it worse. The military desperately needed doctors, but fewer than 100 women doctors were allowed in the armed forces during the war. The WASP pilots who flew for the Army also faced difficulties. They had been hired as civilians, so they had no military insurance. Although they flew as well as men, they earned less than male pilots. Many planes WASPs flew were not in good condition; 38 women pilots lost their lives flying for their country. The Army would not pay to send their coffins home. Fellow WASPs had to collect money to pay for that. In late 1944, as the war started going better, the Army suddenly ended the WASP program. Women would not fly again for the military for nearly 30 years. Because WASPs were civilians, they received no pensions or other benefits after the war.

"If our girls are not good enough to visit their club, then their equipment is not good enough for them [the women] to use. . . .Send every piece of the equipment back. . . . Don't even keep a deck of cards or a pack of ping-pong balls." That order came from the commanding officer of the first African-American WACs to serve overseas, Lieutenant Colonel Charity Adams Earley (shown reviewing her battalion). Her WACs had been going to a Red Cross Club to relax on days off, like other soldiers at the base in England where these women ran the Army post office. But then officials decided black women could not use the club and sent a truckload of recreational equipment for the women to use on their own. She felt that accepting the equipment would mean that this new insult was all right. So she sent it back. She put up with a lot of discrimination to serve her country. But sometimes she just had to speak up.

She was a college graduate in her late 20s. She taught math in her South Carolina hometown before signing up in 1942 as one of the first women to join the Army. When she took over the Army's post office in England in early 1945, she found the postal system was a mess. She reorganized it, and soon her battalion was setting records for speedy delivery. After the war, she left the Army and worked as a college dean. She married, had kids, and wrote a book, *One Woman's Army*. In it she said, "I have opened a few doors, broken a few barriers, and, I hope, smoothed the way to some degree for the next generation."

African-American military women had it tough, too. The armed forces were still segregated. Only the Army made a big effort to sign up black women. More than 4,000 became WACs but could serve only in all-black units. They often faced other discrimination, too. They could not serve overseas until civil rights groups put pressure on the Army. In early 1945, the Army agreed to finally let more than 800 African-American WACs sail to Britain and later to France to run an Army post office. About 500 African Americans also served in the Army Nurse Corps, but only a few were in the Navy Nurse Corps. The Marines had no black women at all. Neither did the WASPs. The WAVES and SPARs let in only a few blacks near the end of the war, but these women made history by being allowed to serve with everyone else, not in segregated units. Women from other minority groups were able to serve without being in segregated units. Segregation in the military soon became a thing of the past for everyone. After the war, in 1948, President Harry Truman signed an order ending racial segregation in the U.S. armed forces.

A year earlier, in 1947, things improved for nurses, too, when they finally became full members of the military. A few years later, female doctors were allowed to be regular members of the armed forces, too. But it was not until 1977 that the unfair treatment of the WASPs ended. That year Congress passed a law that said WASPs should have been considered part of the military. That same law also gave military recognition to the Hello Girls of World War I.

TAKEN PRISONER

Early in the war, in the spring of 1942, U.S. forces in the Philippine Islands were defeated. Thousands of U.S. troops were trapped there when Japan took control. They became POWs—prisoners of war. Among the prisoners were 81 women serving with the military: 66 Army nurses, 11 Navy nurses, 3 Army dietitians, and a physical therapist. They spent from two and a half to three years as POWs. Most were held in Manila, the capital of the Philippines, at Santo Tomas University. The Japanese turned the college into a prison for these women and nearly 4,000 other foreigners. U.S. soldiers were held prisoner elsewhere.

Conditions at Santo Tomas were terrible. Prisoners slept in old classrooms. There was never enough food, clothing, or other supplies. Prisoners could walk around the prison camp, but it was surrounded by a stone wall topped by barbed wire. They organized activities to keep up their spirits. For example, a nurse organized a baseball league. But there was so little food that by the second year people were too weak to play ball anymore.

When Santo Tomas became too crowded, Navy nurses were moved to a nearby prison that was just as bad. By the end of their captivity, prisoners had only one meal a day: a cup of watery vegetable soup or a bowl of rice that often had cockroaches and worms in it. Many prisoners died from disease or lack of food. All of the U.S. military women survived, although some became so weak they could barely walk. What kept them going was helping others. They worked in hospitals set up in the prisons. They had few medicines but did their best to care for other prisoners.

In the fall of 1944, U.S. forces launched attacks to win back the Philippines. In February 1945, they freed all the prisoners. Some of these women suffered the rest of their lives from tuberculosis and other diseases they caught in prison. Six other nurses were held as POWs for much shorter periods: Germans captured an Army flight nurse when the plane she was in was shot down in Germany; and five Navy nurses were taken prisoner by Japan during fighting on the Pacific island of Guam.

NAVY NURSES WHO WERE PRISONERS IN THE PHILIPPINES TALK WITH A U.S. NAVAL OFFICER AFTER BEING RESCUED. THEY HAD SPENT THREE YEARS IN PRISON CAMPS. EACH LATER RECEIVED THE BRONZE STAR, A MEDAL THAT HONORS HEROISM IN THE FACE OF ENEMY ACTION.

SERVING IN THE WAVES LAUNCHED
LIEUTENANT HELEN CLIFFORD GUNTER
ON A NEW CAREER. AS A WAVE, SHE WORKED
IN THE NAVY FILM OFFICE DURING WORLD
WAR II, MAINLY MAKING MOVIES TO TEACH
SAILORS HOW TO BE HOSPITAL CORPSMEN
OR HOW TO REPAIR MACHINES. AS A FORMER
JUNIOR HIGH SCHOOL TEACHER, SHE KNEW
HOW TO CATCH A VIEWER'S INTEREST BY
USING CARTOONS TO MAKE A TRAINING
FILM MORE FUN. IN THIS PHOTO, SHE IS
ON A BOAT IN FLORIDA FILMING NAVY
RESEARCHERS CONDUCTING AN EXPERIMENT
TO TEST A NEW SHARK REPELLENT. THE NAVY
HOPED THE REPELLENT WOULD PROTECT
PEOPLE STRANDED IN THE WATER AFTER
THEIR SHIP SANK. IN THE EXPERIMENT,
RESEARCHERS FIRST ATTRACTED SHARKS
WITH FOOD AND THEN THREW THE REPELLENT
INTO THE OCEAN TO SEE IF IT WOULD DRIVE
THE SHARKS AWAY. IT DID. AFTER THE WAR,
SHE LEFT THE WAVES, MARRIED, AND
STARTED A COMPANY THAT MADE FILMS
FOR SCHOOLS.

ROSIE THE RIVETER

Back home, women once again temporarily took over the jobs of men who went to war. These women, many of whom were married with young children, did a wide range of jobs, from building aircraft and ships to making weapons. There were about six million of these Rosie the Riveters, as they were nicknamed, many more than in earlier wars, because so many more men served in this war than in any other. About 15 million troops served in this war, over seven times more than in World War I. Thousands of civilian women also served as Red Cross volunteers or as performers who entertained the troops. Some women were even spies.

A BIG STEP FORWARD

"There were many bets against you when you first came . . . that you couldn't take it . . . . Everyone who bet against you, lost." That's what Colonel Mary Hallaren wrote after the war in a letter to the WACs she had commanded in Europe. Male commanders also offered praise. General Douglas MacArthur, head of U.S. forces in the Pacific, called WACs "my best soldiers." Besides praise, more than 2,000 women received military awards, including the Air Medal, Distinguished Service Medal, Bronze Star, and the Purple Heart, which is given to those wounded or killed by enemy fire.

When the war ended in 1945 after Germany and Japan surrendered, many people wanted to forget about war and go back to how things were before, when women stayed home and men did most of the paying jobs. Most Rosie the Riveters had to leave their jobs. So did most military women. Many married and became stay-at-home moms, like other 1950s women. But not all women quit working. After the war, the percentage of women who had paying jobs was slightly higher than before the war. Some women, like First Lieutenant Pullman, missed the teamwork they experienced in the military. When her kids were old enough to go to school, she started working again as a part-time nurse in a civilian hospital. First Lieutenant Davis has volunteered as a Red Cross nurse ever since the war ended. Other servicewomen used a benefit that they, like all veterans, received: free college tuition. This helped Lieutenant Colonel Earley earn a master's degree.

The military had planned to close its women's units after the war. But officials began to realize it would be wise to have some women in the military during peacetime as well as in wars. Thanks to pressure from two female members of Congress—Margaret Chase Smith and Edith Nourse Rogers—in 1948, Congress passed a bill that let women become permanent members of the Army, Navy, Marines, and the newly created Air Force. Coast Guard women could not be part of the regular force but could join the Coast Guard Reserves.

There were drawbacks to the new law. It said no more than 2 percent of the armed forces could be female, and women could not rise all the way up in rank. Although nurses could be on military ships and planes during rescue missions, servicewomen could not serve on ships or planes during combat. They would not be allowed in combat on the ground either. Because serving in combat-related jobs increases a person's chances of being promoted, being kept out of those positions limits women's military careers. Even so, servicewomen were glad to have a place on the team. Many signed up as active-duty servicewomen. Others joined the Reserves, ready to be called up in an emergency.

Progress in opening up more opportunities for women would be slow and frustrating during the next few years. But the thousands of military and civilian women who served in World War II proved that women could handle just about any task placed before them. They planted the seeds of change that would blossom with the successes of the women's rights movement of the 1960s and 1970s.

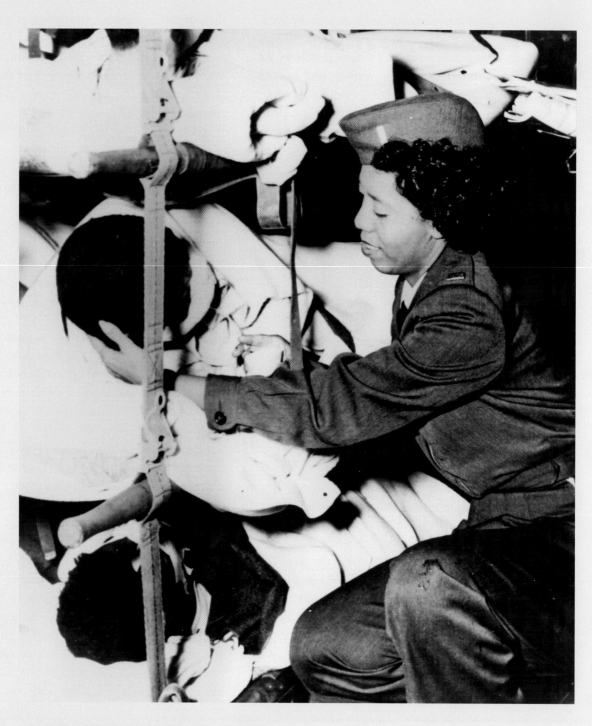

AIR FORCE FLIGHT NURSE FIRST LIEUTENANT A. DRISDALE
HELPS A WOUNDED SOLDIER BEING AIRLIFTED ON A TRANSPORT
PLANE FROM KOREA TO A U.S. MILITARY HOSPITAL IN JAPAN.
THESE PLANES USED MULTI-LEVEL BUNK BEDS.

KOREAN WAR

1950 - 1953

"I had no conception of what we were going to face in Korea. I had no idea that we would get so many patients so fast, for so long," recalled Commander Lura Emery. She was a nurse at a Navy hospital in California when U.S. troops suddenly were sent to Asia to serve in South Korea in the summer of 1950. Soon she was on a hospital ship, the USS *Repose.* It reached South Korea in September, docking at Pusan, on the southern coast. Fighting had started. Wounded U.S. soldiers were brought to her ship by train. Day and night, "they just kept coming," she said. "We were lucky if we got two hours' sleep a night. I never dreamed it would be that bad."

Few people dreamed the U.S. would be in another war so soon after World War II. But the Communist government of North Korea sent troops to invade South Korea in June 1950. The newly created United Nations felt it had to help South Korea to prevent it from being taken over by a Communist dictatorship. The UN sent South Korea a force of troops from 16 countries, including about half a million soldiers from the U.S. At first, this UN force pushed back the invaders. But then thousands of Chinese Communist troops showed up to help North Korea. Fighting continued for three years, until North Korea agreed to leave South Korea alone. The war devastated the countryside and left millions dead, including more than 33,000 U.S. troops.

Since 1948, women had been permanent members of the U.S. armed forces, with about 22,000 on active duty at the start of this war. But they played a smaller role than in World War II. At least 600 Army, Navy, and Air Force nurses served in Korea, where the fighting took place. A few WACs worked at the Army's headquarters in South Korea. But officials would not let other military women serve in Korea at all, fearing the situation was too dangerous for people who did not absolutely have to be there, as nurses did. However, many servicewomen helped with the war by working nearby, at U.S. hospitals and bases in Japan, the Philippines, or Hawaii. Besides nursing and other health care jobs, women did mainly office work, although some Air Force women were air traffic specialists.

Women's more limited role came partly because many fewer troops were involved in Korea than in World War II. The military was not as desperate for more helpers. There was still a 2 percent limit on how many servicepeople could be female. There was also a shift in attitude in the U.S., with many people wanting to go back to days when women did mainly what were thought of as "women's jobs." That was true not just in the civilian world but in the military, too. The path toward increasing opportunities for women has not always been straight and smooth. Women took big steps forward during World War II, but then had to take a few steps back in the 1950s. Yet the outstanding performance of servicewomen in the Korean conflict kept them on track to spring forward again later when attitudes shifted in their favor.

TWO ARMY NURSES (SECOND AND FOURTH FROM RIGHT) POSE WITH OTHER
MEMBERS OF THEIR MASH UNIT. SOME NURSES SERVING IN KOREA HAD ALSO
SERVED IN WORLD WAR II, INCLUDING TWO WHO HAD BEEN PRISONERS OF WAR
IN THE PHILIPPINES. NO AMERICAN NURSES WERE TAKEN PRISONER IN KOREA,
BUT ABOUT 15 LOST THEIR LIVES DURING THIS CONFLICT.

TENTS, SHIPS, AND HELICOPTERS

Army nurses were in South Korea a few days after
the first U.S. troops landed. Many nurses traveled with
the troops, working near the fighting in a new kind of
hospital: a MASH (Mobile Army Surgical Hospital).
Living conditions were just as rough as in earlier wars:
drafty tents, mud, snow, and freezing weather. But some
things were different. MASH operating rooms were
better equipped than frontline hospitals in earlier wars.
Medical care was more advanced. However, the biggest
improvement came from a new invention: the helicopter. In 1951, helicopters began airlifting injured soldiers

from battlefields and delivering them within minutes to MASH hospitals. The sooner patients could be operated on, the better their chances of surviving.

Helicopters also began airlifting the wounded to three Navy hospital ships docked around Korea. After receiving treatment on a hospital ship or at a MASH unit, patients were often flown on transport planes to U.S. military hospitals in Japan. Sometimes hospital ships sailed directly to Japan with a shipload of patients. These ships were like regular hospitals. Their nurses wore traditional nurse's uniforms, rather than the combat pants and boots that MASH nurses wore. The USS *Repose,* where Commander Emery worked, had several operating rooms. It had bunk beds for more than 700 patients who "were so grateful to be aboard the ship and to be in a clean area and to be safe," she said. "We just did everything we could to keep them alive and get them back home." She worked long hours but still kept up her spirits—even when she had lice! She became infested with those creepy, crawly insects from her patients. During battles, the soldiers often had to sleep on the ground or in muddy trenches, with no chance to wash. Some injured soldiers were covered with lice when they reached her ship. As she cleaned them up, some lice crawled onto her. It is hard to get rid of them. It took her three weeks. When patients heard she had lice, they "would just hoop and howl and have a good time. It was something that relieved the stress."

CAPTAIN CARMELA FILOSA HIX

"I always wanted to be a nurse. When I was little, I played nurse with my dolls," said Captain Carmela Filosa Hix (third from the left in this photo of her MASH unit). After high school in New York, she went to nursing school. Then she became the first in her family to go to a university. There, she had more training as a nurse. When U.S. troops went to Korea, she left a job at a New York hospital to join the Army. "This country meant a lot to me. My parents had immigrated here from Italy. I felt I should give something back because this country had been so good to my family."

Her first night as an operating room nurse at a MASH hospital unit in Korea was tough. "Before then my patients had been elderly," she said. At the MASH unit, her patients were young men with terrible injuries. That night "was the only time I cried. I didn't let them see it. I went outside and cried. I thought, 'I don't know if I can handle this.' I went to my tent, sat on the bed, and prayed. I got my courage back. After that I couldn't let myself get too emotional or I wouldn't be any use as a nurse."

Some days would be very busy. When helicopters brought in lots of patients, she would work day and night until all the patients had been operated on and sent off by plane to recover at a military hospital in Japan. During less busy times, doctors would sometimes goof off to release tension. "Their sense of humor kept up our spirits. But they were excellent surgeons." After the war, she stayed in the Army for several years, even after marrying. But when she had her first child, she had to leave the Army. "At that time, you couldn't be in the service and have children."

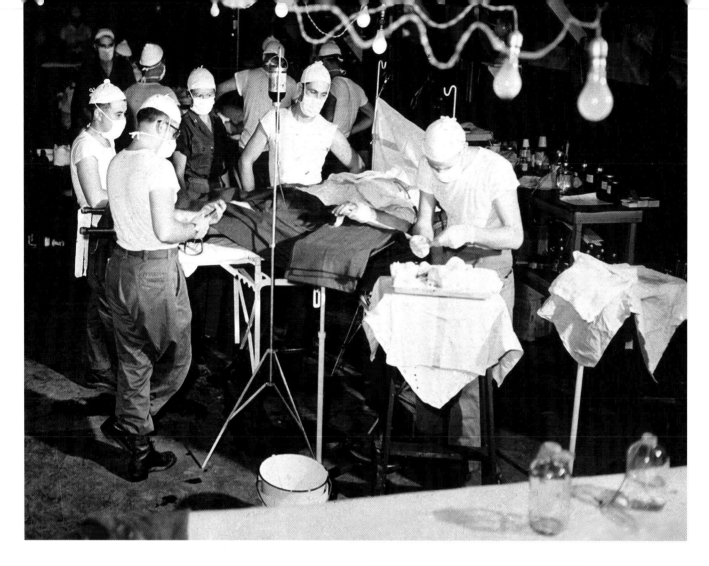

NURSES ASSIST DOCTORS OPERATING ON A PATIENT IN AN OPERATING ROOM OF A MASH UNIT.

GETTING ALONG

Something else was new in this war besides helicopters. Since 1948, segregation was no longer the official policy of the armed forces, although some units integrated faster than others. Even so, a great many African Americans were able to serve alongside everyone else in Korea. Shortly after this war, the integration of the entire force was complete. This was a welcome change for First Lieutenant Evelyn Decker, who became an Army nurse near the end of World War II. She had been upset by the discrimination she faced when her unit was still segregated. But in Korea, she and another black nurse served alongside 17 white nurses in a MASH unit. Only one white nurse had trouble with the new situation. As for the rest, "We got along fabulously," First Lieutenant Decker recalled. Of course, there were still some prejudiced people on duty, but at least official segregation was coming to an end.

"I found that everyone was people," said Private First Class Muriel Scharrer Wimmer. Until being placed in one of the WAC's first integrated basic training units, this 20-year-old New Yorker had not had much contact with African Americans or other people from backgrounds different from her own. During the Korean War, she worked at an Army hospital in Japan as a medic, someone who helps the nurses. She said that at first "I kind of resented the Japanese because of World War II." She changed after getting to know Japanese people who worked for the Army. In the hospital, she took care of soldiers from some of the other countries in the UN force. One of her favorite patients was a young man from the African country of Ethiopia. Although he spoke no English, they managed to communicate and became friends. She learned to "judge people as individuals, not by their color or race."

STAFF SERGEANT ERNESTINE JOHNSON THOMAS

"I had less problem with racism in the military than in the civilian world," said Staff Sergeant Ernestine Johnson Thomas (shown here at her desk at Air Force headquarters in Japan during the Korean War). She was one of the few African Americans working in that office, which ordered supplies the Air Force used in the war. She became friends with her nonblack co-workers. "Our friendships were above and beyond race. We were in a foreign situation away from home. We supported each other." At age 20, she was one of the three youngest in the office. "The rest of the women mothered us," she recalled.

"We felt that what we were doing was important," she said. One of her first assignments was typing reports about pilots shot down in Korea. "Those reports made me feel that this was very serious business." She also learned a lot by seeing "how other people lived who hadn't lived in the same environment I had." She came from a small midwestern town where her high school did not give her information about going to college. So she enlisted in the Air Force. She gained a lot of self-confidence serving overseas. "The military helped me understand the broader side of the world." She left the Air Force after three years and went to college. Later, she married, had kids, and held administrative jobs at several universities.

FORGOTTEN WAR

"When we came back from Korea, no one asked where we were, what we had done," said Commander Emery. "No one wanted to hear about the war." Most of the returning troops received the same reaction. That's why many call this the "Forgotten War." She felt that "people in the States were just so fed up with war that they didn't want to know about what was going on." Many people were also disappointed that there was no formal peace treaty to end the Korean War. Instead, in 1953 when the fighting stopped, North and South Korea set up a neutral zone between them to make it harder for either side to attack. Some U.S. troops stayed there to keep Communists from invading again. Although veterans felt ignored by the public, military officials praised servicewomen and awarded many of them medals for bravery. Quite a few women received the Bronze Star, including First Lieutenant Decker and other nurses in her MASH unit.

Despite this praise, women's roles in the military grew even more limited after the war. The 1950s were a frustrating time for women, both in and out of the military. In the civilian world, at least women could try for a career if they were determined, and a few made it into professions that used to be mainly for men, such as law, medicine, and engineering. But in the armed forces, officials would not let women even try for most military jobs. The main military jobs open to women were office jobs, nursing, or other medically oriented work. They could not be pilots or serve on ships. Nor could they rise all the way up in rank. There definitely were no female generals or admirals.

Servicewomen were still called WACs, WAVES, SPARs, and WAFs (Women in the Air Force), which set them apart and made them seem different from the men. The hardest restriction was the no-kids rule. Servicewomen could marry, but if they became pregnant or adopted children, they had to leave the military. These women had to choose between being a mom or having a military career.

Many dedicated women worked all through the 1950s and 1960s to improve conditions for servicewomen. Their efforts started to pay off in the late 1960s. By then, the country was in a new war that deeply divided the nation but that also led to big changes for women in the military.

CAPTAIN ELIZABETH FINN WAS ONE OF MANY ARMY NURSES IN
THE VIETNAM WAR WHO TOOK CARE OF VIETNAMESE CHILDREN
AS WELL AS WOUNDED SOLDIERS. HERE SHE IS CHECKING THE
EYES OF A CHILD AT A VIETNAMESE ORPHANAGE.

VIETNAM WAR

1959 - 1975

A young Army major named Colin Powell made himself a promise after serving in the 1960s in the Vietnam War: He wanted to keep the U.S. from ever being in a war like that again. In his autobiography, *My American Journey,* he described that war as "halfhearted warfare for half-baked reasons that the American people could not understand or support." He felt the U.S. should fight only for "a purpose that our people understand and support; we should mobilize the country's resources to fulfill that mission and then go in to win." He did his best to keep his promise years later when he became a four-star general and then Secretary of State. However, the Vietnam War did more than change the way generals handled future conflicts. It totally changed the role of women in the military.

Only a few kinds of military jobs were open to women in 1959 when the U.S. started becoming involved in Vietnam. By 1975, when this war ended, servicewomen were beginning to have a much wider range of jobs. There were even a few female brigadier generals and rear admirals by then.

These changes happened partly because this war was so unpopular. The military had trouble using the draft, its usual way to round up troops. Since World War II, men age 18 and up had to register for the draft. Each year, a certain number of men were "drafted"—told they had to join the military whether they wanted to or

not. In the early 1960s, small numbers of drafted men were sent to South Vietnam to try to keep it from being taken over by the Communist North Vietnamese. Most Americans supported this effort at first. But the disputes among the Vietnamese could not be solved quickly. Year after year, more U.S. men were drafted to fight there. In 1967, nearly half a million U.S. troops were bogged down in Vietnam. More than two million would serve there by the time this longest war in U.S. history ended in 1975. About 58,000 Americans lost their lives, as did more than a million Vietnamese. By the late 1960s, many Americans no longer understood why U.S. troops were there. A growing number of people did not want more men drafted for this war.

To hold down the number who had to be drafted, officials in the late 1960s decided to have more women do noncombat jobs. To help this plan succeed, in 1967 the military started to make a series of changes that gradually made military service more attractive and fair for women. Officials hoped this would encourage women to enlist. The military was catching up with the civilian world, where the women's rights movement was gaining strength. By the late 1960s, more women were going to college and nearly half of all U.S. women had paying jobs. Civilian women were speaking up for more equality of opportunity. Servicewomen began speaking up for their rights, too.

STRUGGLING TO SERVE

"What kind of delicate creatures do the brass think we are?" That quote from an Army WAC appeared in a magazine in the mid-1960s. She was frustrated because many male commanders would not send servicewomen to Vietnam. At first officials followed the same policy as in the Korean War and let only nurses serve in Vietnam. Things began to change when the commander of all U.S. forces in Vietnam became unhappy with the way male soldiers handled office work at his headquarters. He had a few women from the WACs brought over to Vietnam to work in his office. Eventually about 1,100 servicewomen who were not nurses served in Vietnam or in other nearby Southeast Asian countries where the American forces had bases.

For most of the war, these women did mainly office jobs: typing reports, writing articles for military publications, taking care of military finances, or keeping track of where soldiers were stationed. The changes that started opening up more kinds of jobs to servicewomen did not go into effect until near the end of the war. Even so, women contributed a lot. The office jobs women did were essential to ensuring the smooth running of military headquarters and command centers. Specialist Doris Allen had an especially important job. This African American had been in the WACs for more than 15 years. She studied reports about enemy activities so that American commanders could make better plans for their troops.

NURSES HELP WITH AN OPERATION AT AN ARMY HOSPITAL IN VIETNAM DURING THE WAR.

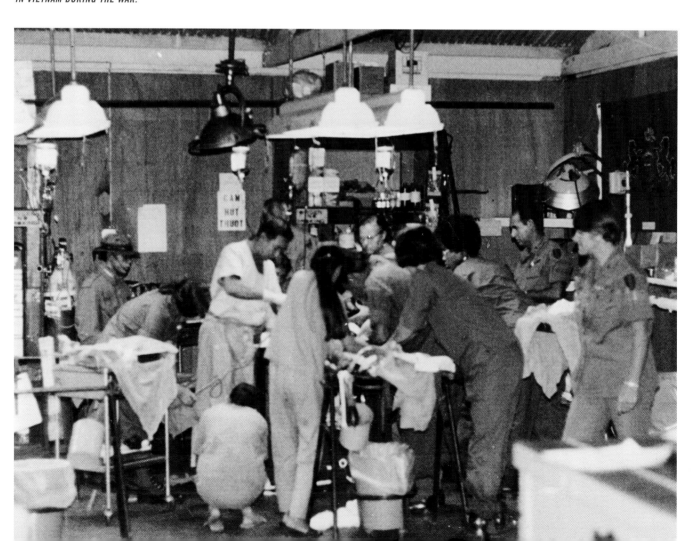

"When I came home, who was there to talk to who would understand? Nobody wanted to hear," said First Lieutenant Lily Lee Adams. She was describing what it was like to come home in the fall of 1970 after a year as an Army nurse in Vietnam. She thought people would praise her for risking her life to help over there. She had taken care of soldiers and also injured Vietnamese children. "My job was to save them," she said. There were no groups to help nurses or other veterans deal with their feelings. "You were all by yourself," she said. "You just wanted to forget it."

She left the Army, worked as a nurse in civilian hospitals, married, and had two kids. But she could not forget Vietnam. About 10 years later, certain things made her very upset, such as hearing a helicopter, a sound she heard a lot in Vietnam. That sound brought back bad memories. She was having PTSD (post-traumatic stress disorder). Luckily she met people who helped her deal with her feelings.

In 1982 she went to the dedication of a memorial for Vietnam veterans in Washington, D.C. "There were thousands of veterans there. Everybody talked to everybody. People were crying. That opened things up for me." Male veterans she did not even know thanked her for helping in Vietnam. She began to feel proud of what she did there and became active in veterans groups, counseling others with PTSD. In 1997, she brought her daughter to the new Women's Memorial *(see page 7)* so she could see that "women had served their country."

TAKING CARE

Nurses were the largest group of American servicewomen in Vietnam. Over the course of the war, about 6,000 nurses served there, working in emergency hospitals, base hospitals, or hospital ships. Air Force nurses worked mainly as flight nurses, airlifting wounded to military hospitals in the U.S., Vietnam, or other Asian countries. Living conditions were often better than in earlier wars, with some air-conditioned buildings. But the sadness of seeing so many injured young men was the same.

Unlike in other wars, servicewomen and men did not serve for the whole war. A tour of duty was one year, although some served more than one tour. One year in Vietnam could seem like a long time. Danger was everywhere. No place was safe from bombings or terrorist attacks. Four Navy nurses were injured when a car bomb damaged the building where they lived in South Vietnam's capital city. They received Purple Hearts for bravery. Enemy rockets destroyed part of a hospital at a U.S. base where Vietnamese women and children were being treated. An Army nurse, First Lieutenant Sharon Lane, died in this attack. This 25-year-old was the only U.S. nurse to die in this war from enemy fire. About seven others also lost their lives, mainly in plane crashes.

Besides the Purple Heart, servicewomen received Bronze Stars and other honors. However, many felt disappointed when they came home. People in the U.S. did not want to hear about the war. This was partly because so many people, including some Vietnam veterans, were upset about this war. So nurses and other veterans did not talk much about their wartime experiences. Some became depressed or were bothered by bad dreams. Soldiers in earlier wars had sometimes felt this way, but the emotional pain felt by so many Vietnam veterans helped health professionals understand more about this condition: post-traumatic stress disorder (PTSD). Luckily experts now have found ways to treat PTSD, mainly by having a person speak with a trained counselor. Today the military has Combat Stress Teams with counselors who help people deal with what they might experience in war.

CAPTAIN JULIA BARNES

"I saw the stress of war at the Naval Hospital in Philadelphia," said Captain Julia Barnes. She was there in the operating rooms during most of the Vietnam War. Thousands of troops wounded in combat were airlifted there for surgery and rehabilitation. She saw another side of war in 1975 when she became Chief Nurse at the Naval Hospital in Guam, an island in the South Pacific. That year, as North Vietnamese Communists took over South Vietnam, thousands of South Vietnamese escaped. U.S. helicopters brought out many of these refugees. Others escaped on small, rickety ships. Most came first to Guam, where tents were set up all over the island. She and her nurses worked day and night caring for refugees who were sick.

She was the first in her family to go on for higher education and a professional career. "I was the first black nurse sent overseas to be a Chief Nurse," she said. "But being black was not an issue. I had the experience and qualifications for the job, could handle crisis situations, and was selected for that assignment." By then she had been in the Navy more than 15 years. She stayed in the Navy for another 16 years, tackling other senior leadership positions, including being one of the first women put in charge of a Navy Medical Center.

CHANGING TIMES

A lot changed during the 1960s. The civil rights movement led to new laws that made it illegal to discriminate against people, no matter what their race or gender. The women's rights movement led to more people feeling it was all right for women to have careers, including married women with kids. These new attitudes, combined with the antidraft feelings on the home front, led to big changes for servicewomen, too.

The first thing to change was the old law that said no more than 2 percent of military people could be female. This had to change so the military could sign up more women and draft fewer men. In 1967, Congress passed a new law that put no limit on how many women could join or on the ranks they could achieve. The Army had its first female brigadier general by 1970. In 1972, the Navy had its first female rear admiral. The Coast Guard no longer signed up women just in the Reserves but let women serve in the regular force, too.

In 1973, there was another major change: The draft ended. Men no longer were required to serve. By then,

the U.S. had signed an agreement with North Vietnam. U.S. troops were coming home, although fighting continued among the Vietnamese for two more years. The U.S. military became an all-volunteer force. That made officials realize how much they would need women. What if not enough men volunteered? Officials began to realize they needed to do more to encourage women to join the armed forces.

Servicewomen actually helped speed up these changes by filing lawsuits. A few lawsuits said it was unfair that women could not stay in the military if they had children after signing up. So in 1975 the military let women serve who had kids. Another lawsuit said it was unfair to keep Navy women off ships, other than hospital ships. Not doing ship duty hurt a woman's chances for promotion. A federal judge agreed. So in 1978 the Navy started letting women serve on noncombat ships. None of the Coast Guard's ships were combat ships, so women could serve on all its ships. Ships built with sleeping space only for men had to be fixed up with separate areas for females.

The Navy also had to adjust to sailors using more water. On all-male ships, sailors did not always take showers every day. Many female sailors have a different attitude about this and tend to shower and wash their hair every day. Once women were on board, the men started washing up more, too. What a difference this was from the Revolutionary War days of Deborah Samson when not many troops bothered to bathe at all!

The skies also opened up to women. In 1973, women could finally train to be Army and Navy pilots. In 1976, they could fly for the Air Force, too. All through the 1970s and 1980s, more and more military jobs slowly

WOMEN QUICKLY MOVED INTO COMMAND POSITIONS AFTER THE RULES CHANGED AND WOMEN COULD SERVE ON SHIPS. IN 1979 LIEUTENANT JUNIOR GRADE BEVERLY KELLEY OF THE COAST GUARD (BELOW) BECAME THE FIRST WOMAN TO COMMAND A U.S. MILITARY SHIP, A 95-FOOT COAST GUARD CUTTER PATROL BOAT.

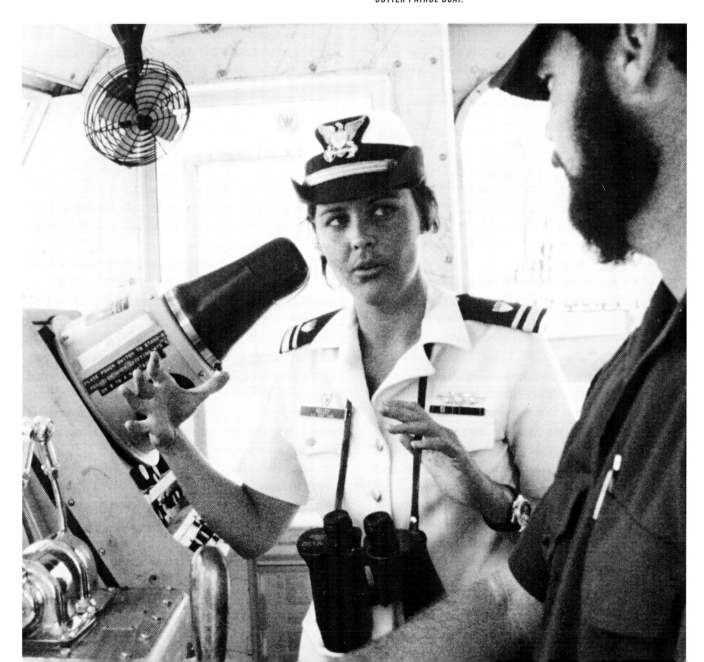

One of the refugees who escaped in 1975 from Vietnam, as the war there finally ended, was Captain Theresa Nguyen. At the time, she was a frightened five-year-old. Nguyen was airlifted out by a helicopter with her sister, two brothers, aunt, and grandmother. They went to refugee camps in the Philippines, Guam, and then to one in Florida for several months. She finally settled in California where she was reunited with her parents. She decided to be like the doctors and nurses who took care of her in the refugee camps. After college, she won an Army scholarship for medical school and became an Army doctor. She likes being an Army doctor because it is "a way for me to give something back to this country." On September 11, 2001, she was on duty at the Pentagon, the military's headquarters near Washington, D.C., caring for people who were injured that day when terrorists hijacked a plane and crashed it into the Pentagon, killing more than a hundred people *(see Chapter 9).*

opened up to women. By the end of the 1980s, combat jobs were just about the only ones still off-limits. The Army was even giving women weapons training—not for combat, but so women could do guard duty and serve in the military police.

In 1976, women were admitted for the first time to the academies that prepare officers: the Naval, Coast Guard, and Air Force Academies, as well as the Army's academy, known as West Point. By then, women were also in Reserve Officers Training Corps (ROTC) programs offered at colleges; these programs give students military training during college so they can be military officers after graduation.

In 1978, the Army finally stopped calling its women WACs. Other branches had already stopped using names like WAVES or SPARs. Now servicewomen became known simply as soldiers, sailors, airmen, and Marines. All these changes paid off: By the end of the 1970s, there were more than 100,000 servicewomen on duty, three times more than in the mid-1960s.

However, there were still some rough spots. "There were times when the men just had to top the women pilots' flying skills so the men would know they were still the 'ace of the base.' But most men wanted us to do well. It was only a minority that caused any friction," said Commander Lucy Young, one of the Navy's first female pilots. She left the military later to be an airline pilot. Command Sergeant Major Mary Sutherland recalled one of her first jobs in the early 1970s, as a 21-year-old supply sergeant for an all-male Army unit. "Everybody was watching to be sure I could do it," she said, "especially in the morning when it would be time for the unit run. They'd run a little farther than usual, hoping I'd drop out. Ten people could fall out, nine could be guys and one could be a woman. Everybody would say, 'Did you see that woman fall out?' They wouldn't mention the nine men."

Servicewomen hung in there and did their best. In 1984, a woman graduated at the top of the class at the Naval Academy. Soon women did the same at the Coast Guard Academy and the Air Force Academy. When war broke out a few years later in the sands of the Persian Gulf, women were trained and ready to go.

AS MORE MILITARY JOBS OPENED UP TO WOMEN AFTER THE VIETNAM WAR, MORE KINDS OF TRAINING OPENED TO THEM AS WELL. THIS PHOTO FROM 1980 SHOWS ARMY SPECIALIST THERESA PHARMS GOING THROUGH WHAT IS KNOWN AS THE GREEN HELL OBSTACLE COURSE, PART OF AN INTENSIVE THREE WEEK TRAINING COURSE THAT HER UNIT UNDERWENT IN PANAMA. SHE WAS THE FIRST SERVICE-WOMAN TO COMPLETE THIS VERY DIFFICULT COURSE.

STAFF SERGEANT KAREN FULCE CHECKS OUT BOMBS
THAT WILL BE LOADED ONTO F-16 FIGHTING FALCON
AIRCRAFT DURING THE PERSIAN GULF WAR.

7

PERSIAN GULF WAR

1990 - 1991

"I was completely clear in my focus about what we were doing, why we were there. I was well trained. I was ready," said Army helicopter pilot Captain Celia FlorCruz. She was talking about her service in the Persian Gulf War in the early 1990s. Also ready were more than 40,000 other U.S. women who served with her, about half of whom were African Americans. In this war, about half a million U.S. troops worked with forces from 27 other countries to make Iraq pull out of Kuwait. Iraq had invaded this country in August 1990. Captain FlorCruz was proud to be part of this effort "to intervene on behalf of peoples wronged by others."

She graduated from the Army's military academy at West Point, in one of the first classes to have women. Then she became a helicopter pilot, a job that had been off-limits to women a few years earlier. In this war, servicewomen did many other jobs that used to be closed to them. Although they still could not take part in combat operations, they were an important part of the team by then, making up more than 11 percent of the armed forces. There had been a few small military operations in the 1980s in which women participated, including one in Panama. But the Persian Gulf War was the first major use of troops since so many new positions opened to women. Men of lesser rank had to take orders from new female officers like Captain FlorCruz. She was second-in-command of a medevac unit that airlifted the injured to safety.

She arrived in Saudi Arabia in September 1990. Her unit joined hundreds of thousands of troops who took part in Operation Desert Shield, the first stage of this mission. They set up bases in the Saudi desert, as officials tried to persuade Iraq to pull out of Kuwait. When Iraq refused, the second stage began in January 1991: Operation Desert Storm. U.S. planes bombed Iraq for about five weeks. Then on February 24, troops moved forward, up through the Saudi desert into Kuwait and Iraq. By then, many Iraqi troops were ready to surrender. The war ended four days later.

"When the action starts . . . ," noted Captain Cynthia Mosley, "nobody cares whether you're male or female. It's just: 'can you do the job?'" She commanded a unit that brought supplies to combat troops in the desert. She and the other women in this war not only did their jobs, but did them "magnificently," according to General H. Norman Schwarzkopf, head of U.S. forces. He and other officials saw that having women serve side by side with men did not hurt a unit's performance. Women earned Bronze Stars, Purple Hearts, and other medals in this war. That helped after the war in winning for servicewomen the right to tackle even more tasks, including some that involved combat.

DELIVERING THE GOODS

Being kept out of combat missions did not mean that the jobs servicewomen did were unimportant. A fighting force needs a huge backup team to provide food, clean water, ammunition, spare parts, and other supplies. A military that runs out of supplies cannot fight. That used to be a big problem, but by the 1990s, the military knew how to provide troops with what was needed.

The backup team also has other jobs to do, such as flying or sailing troops where they need to go; guarding barracks, bases, and ports; setting up hospitals; providing telephones and other communication systems at bases and in battle zones; repairing, servicing, and fueling tanks, trucks, ships, planes, and other equipment; and keeping track of where everyone is so new troops can be brought in as needed. These jobs were done by women in the Persian Gulf War. Of course, men served on the backup team, too. In fact, many men in the armed forces never take part in combat.

Captain Christina Richter Listermann commanded quite a few men in the supply platoon she led. Some of its 40 members were female, but most were male. "If there was any resistance to me it was for being young and inexperienced rather than because I was a woman," said Captain Listermann, who was a 23-year-old recent West Point graduate when she commanded this platoon. "I had people working for me from all different backgrounds and had to learn how to get everybody to work together, to keep cool heads and get the job done."

CAPTAIN CHRISTINA RICHTER LISTERMANN IS STANDING BY ONE OF THE MILITARY VEHICLES USED BY THE PLATOON SHE COMMANDED DURING THE PERSIAN GULF WAR. HER PLATOON KEPT A FIGHTING BRIGADE OF ABOUT 7,000 SOLDIERS SUPPLIED WITH FOOD, FUEL, AND WATER. HER FATHER HAD BEEN IN THE ARMY. SO HAD HER MOTHER, AS A NURSE IN THE 1960s.

"I always wanted to be a pilot," said helicopter pilot Captain Celia FlorCruz. She also always wanted to be an Army officer, like her father. He was from the Philippines and went to West Point Military Academy as an exchange student, graduating in 1942. By then, World War II had started, and Japan had taken over his country. So he joined the U.S. Army. She grew up on Army bases where he worked after the war. She graduated from West Point 40 years after her father, becoming an officer and, a few years later, a pilot, too.

The Persian Gulf War offered one of her toughest challenges as a pilot. The fine desert sand in Saudi Arabia can swirl around an aircraft during takeoff and landing, messing up the engine and making it hard to see. Also tough was living in a tent in the desert. "One of the first things I did was cut off my long hair," she said. "I knew water would be a problem and washing long hair takes a lot of water." At her unit's base camp, there was a shower. But when her unit moved forward with the troops to fly missions over Iraq, there were no more showers and little chance to wash. Going to the bathroom was tricky. "It's all flat so you can't even duck behind a hill for a little privacy. You can, however, put your rain poncho on and squat down inside it," she explained.

A few years after the war, she left the active-duty force to be in the Reserves. Early in her career, she kept by her desk a photo of the WASP pilots of World War II *(see page 39)*. "If I grew discouraged, the enthusiasm in the WASPs' faces lifted me right back up. I'd say to myself, 'If they could do it, I can, too!'"

THE MOMMY WAR

Many servicewomen in the Persian Gulf War were moms. By 1990, it was no longer unusual for moms in the civilian world to work. More than half of U.S. women had paying jobs by then, including more than half of all mothers with young kids. Moms who served in the Persian Gulf War, such as Captain FlorCruz, had to arrange for their kids to be cared for back home, often by the father, grandparents, or other relatives. Having so many moms serving in a war zone was a first. Newspapers and magazines called it the "Mommy War."

While Captain FlorCruz was away, her husband took care of their young daughter at their home in North Carolina. It was hard for troops to phone home during this war. There was no e-mail yet for the troops. So she wrote letters home every day, and recorded cassette tapes and a video to send, too. Luckily she returned safely after seven months, arriving home two days before her daughter's second birthday

Some people worried about whether kids really had good care while parents served in this war. In a few cases, *both* parents of a child served in the Persian Gulf War. Most military moms and dads made good child-care plans. But after the war, the military issued new rules that would allow mothers of very young babies to choose whether or not to go when units went overseas. Other new rules required that parents set up good child-care plans. This was especially important for single moms—and single dads. (There are actually more single dads than single moms in the military.) The fact that the military was working so hard to help mothers serve overseas in wartime, as fathers had for so many years, showed how much things were changing.

WAITING FOR A CALL

"I got a phone call on a Saturday night from a commanding officer who said I needed to report the next morning," recalled Chief Petty Officer Mary Fowlkes. She was in the Coast Guard Reserves and was being called up to serve in the Persian Gulf War. Reservists were a large part of the total number of people who served in this war. Reservists usually have other jobs in the civilian world and put in just a few weekend days of service a month with their Reserve unit, plus a few weeks each summer. Their units are usually based near their homes. But during wars or other emergencies, Reserve units can be "called up." When that happens, the people in those units have to go wherever the military sends them. Their employers have to hold their jobs for them until the military lets their Reserve units return home again.

It was September when Chief Petty Officer Fowlkes received her telephone call-up for the Persian Gulf War. She was a physical education teacher at a Wisconsin middle school. Because she was single, with no kids, she did not suddenly have to find child care, but her school had to find a substitute for her classes. She phoned her principal right away. Then she was off to Saudi Arabia, where she was one of six women working with 85 men in a Coast Guard Port Security unit. Its boats guarded a

Saudi port. "My job was to arrange to purchase anything people needed, from oil for the boats' engines to nails and pencils."

However, if things had to be bought at a local Saudi store, she did not do the buying because Saudis did not approve of women doing that. Male co-workers handled store trips. She never went to town without a man, and when in town, wore a uniform or long pants and a long-sleeved shirt because Saudis think women should cover their bodies. When her unit returned home after six months, hundreds of people—including a busload of her students—came to the airport to welcome the Reservists home. Warm welcome-home gatherings and parades greeted many returning Gulf War troops, a big change from the indifference and even hostility that greeted many Vietnam veterans years earlier when they had returned home.

CHIEF PETTY OFFICER MARY FOWLKES (FAR RIGHT PHOTO) STANDS ON ONE OF THE COAST GUARD BOATS THAT PROVIDED PORT SECURITY DURING THE PERSIAN GULF WAR. WHEN HER UNIT CAME HOME TO WISCONSIN AFTER SIX MONTHS IN THE PERSIAN GULF, HER FAMILY (NEAR RIGHT) WAS PART OF THE LARGE WELCOME-HOME CROWD AT THE AIRPORT.

"I drove a two-and-a-half-ton armored truck and then another armored vehicle that we used for medical supplies. I drove a car at home, but didn't have training in how to drive a military vehicle. When I got out to the desert they said, 'This is your vehicle. Drive it.' So I learned," said Staff Sergeant Kim Chambers, an Army medic in the Persian Gulf War. She was 18 years old, right out of high school. Of three soldiers and a doctor on her team, she was the only female. "They used to play jokes at first, asking me to find things that didn't exist," she said. "But I carried my own weight. I gained their respect."

Right before the ground war began, her medical vehicle went with the troops as they drove through the desert toward Iraq. At night, the tanks and other vehicles lined up in columns. Everyone dug his or her own bunker hole in the sand between the vehicles. "The hole had to be deep enough to be six inches above your nose if you were on your back. We slept in the holes, but sand blew into your hole so you never got much sleep," she recalled. When the fighting started, her vehicle would stop to treat wounded soldiers. Sometimes it was fired on. "Then we got out, put the vehicle between us and where the fire was coming from, dug a hole and got down into it, in fight position. Tanks would fire in the direction the fire came from." She is part of the "enlisted" force, people who do not start as officers but can rise in rank. She started as a private and has become a staff sergeant. She has also earned a college degree while in the Army, paid for by the Army.

CHANGING MINDS

Many women who served in the Persian Gulf War entered the armed forces in the early 1980s, a time when some military men were unhappy about having so many females in the force. "It was still very anti-woman with some people back then," recalled Navy Commander Susan Fink, who was at the Naval Academy in the early 1980s. Negative remarks hurt, but she said she "realized there are more good people in the Navy than those guys. You deal with it. You try to have a sense of humor. You put the mission higher than your feelings." Negative comments fired up some women to do better. Captain Julie DelGiorno decided, "I'm going to be successful because they don't think I should be here." That helped at West Point and in the Persian Gulf War, during which she earned a Bronze Star. "I wanted to do well because I didn't want them to use the excuse of 'Oh, she's a woman. She can't do it.'"

Women who served in this war won over many doubters.

Soon after the fighting stopped, Lieutenant Commander Kristen Fabry served in the Mediterranean Sea on a Navy supply ship that resupplied ships that were on patrol to make sure Iraq kept the terms of the peace agreement. She reported:

"There were a few men who would work with you completely professionally and then you'd find out that they really didn't think women should be out there. Not all the men, just a very small percentage. But when I questioned them more deeply, they did have to admit that some of the best officers on board ship were women. They realized that when we worked side by side, we were doing more than our share of the work and showing great leadership traits. You really have to work hard, but if you do, you can gain their respect."

AIR FORCE CAPTAIN BONNIE VAN DYKE (INSET) IS AT THE CONTROLS OF A KC-135R TANKER PLANE SHE FLEW TO REFUEL PLANES IN THE AIR DURING THE PERSIAN GULF WAR. HERE, A KC-135R STRATOTANKER IS REFUELING AN F-15C EAGLE FIGHTER PLANE ON COMBAT PATROL DURING OPERATION DESERT SHIELD, THE FIRST PART OF THE PERSIAN GULF WAR. TO DELIVER THE FUEL, A TANKER PILOT HAS TO POSITION THE LARGE TANKER PLANE OVER THE OTHER PLANE AND THEN LOWER A STIFF TUBE CALLED A BOOM INTO AN OPENING ON THE TOP OF THE OTHER PLANE. THEN FUEL FROM THE TANKER PLANE FLOWS THROUGH THE BOOM INTO THE OTHER AIRCRAFT'S FUEL TANK.

SHOT DOWN

On the next-to-last day of the Persian Gulf War, Colonel Rhonda Cornum, an Army doctor, was the only female on board an Army Black Hawk helicopter. It was flying over the Iraqi desert to try to rescue an injured Air Force pilot. Her helicopter was shot down. Five of the chopper's crew members died in the crash. She was hurt badly, with two broken arms, a smashed-up knee, and an injured shoulder with a bullet in it. But she survived. So did two other crew members. All three were taken prisoner by Iraqi troops.

The possibility of women becoming prisoners was one reason officials did not want women in combat, for fear that they might be abused or might not be able to handle the stress. An Iraqi guard tried to abuse Colonel Cornum, but her fierce screams stopped him. Most of the other Iraqis treated her fairly well. She was in pain and had no idea how long she would be held, but she was determined to keep up her spirits. She sang rock songs very loudly in her prison cell, to cheer up herself and other POWs who might be nearby—and also, perhaps, to annoy her guards. Iraqis questioned her but she refused to tell secret information. She knew how to handle herself in risky situations. After all, she was someone who liked to skydive back home, just for fun. As her teenage daughter told reporters, "My mother is not a wimp."

Another woman who was not a wimp had been taken prisoner several weeks earlier. Specialist Fourth Class Melissa Rathbun-Nealy Coleman and a male soldier were captured as they drove an Army truck through the desert. She was treated fairly well during her 33 days as a POW. About a week after the war ended, she and Colonel Cornum were freed from prison. Both were awarded Purple Hearts.

Major Marie T. Rossi was not so lucky. An Army helicopter pilot, she flew many missions over Iraq during the Persian Gulf War, delivering soldiers, ammunition, and other supplies. Just before troops moved into Iraq, CNN broadcast an interview with her on TV. She was upbeat and told the interviewer it was no big deal for a woman to do what she did. She said that "this is the moment that everybody trains for—that I've trained for—so I feel ready to meet the challenge." On the day after the fighting stopped, she had to make another flight. It was at night. The weather was bad. There was a communications tower up ahead that she could not see because it was not lit up. Her Chinook helicopter hit the tower and she died in the crash. Altogether about 150 American troops lost their lives in this war, including more than a dozen women. Hundreds of thousands of Iraqis and Kuwaitis also died.

THE SKY'S THE LIMIT

During the Persian Gulf War, people realized that some reasons for keeping women out of combat no longer made sense. One reason had been to keep women safe. But women had been in danger in every war in which they served. In this war, three of the servicewomen who died were working far from the battlefront. They died when an Iraqi missile hit their barracks.

Another reason for the no-combat rule was the idea that females were not strong enough. But war had changed since the hand-to-hand fighting days of earlier wars. Much of modern warfare involves no direct contact with the enemy at all. This is especially true of work on combat planes and ships, which requires intelligence and skill, not great physical strength.

Many of the so-called noncombat jobs that women did in this war seemed like they were part of combat. An African-American lieutenant, Phoebe Jeter, commanded an all-male Patriot missile unit. She ordered missiles to be fired to knock down Iraqi missiles before they hit U.S. troops. Some women were in the air during bombing raids, working on special aircraft that helped select targets for bomber pilots. Other women piloted KC-135 jet tankers in order to refuel the bombers.

In addition, some female Navy pilots were already flying fighter and bomber aircraft, just not in combat missions. By not letting women fly real combat missions, the military was losing the help of some very talented pilots. It was also hurting the women's careers. Combat duty increases a person's chances of being promoted. Officials realized some of the most outstanding women might not stay in the military long if there were so many limitations on what they could achieve.

So in 1991 Congress decided that women could fly combat missions. In 1993, Congress voted to let women serve on most Navy combatant ships, too, except submarines and a few specialty ships. The Army began opening more jobs also. Servicewomen could not engage in direct combat, such as serve in infantry, artillery, commando, or armored tank units. But they could do just about anything else.

COMMANDER SUSAN FINK

"I always wanted to drive a battleship," said Navy Commander Susan Fink, whose father and older brother were Navy officers who drove ships. She graduated from the Naval Academy in 1986 when combatant ships were still off-limits to women. But she heard of a way to get around the no-combat rule: Be a helicopter pilot. A pilot could be stationed on a combatant ship, without being listed officially as part of the ship's crew. So she became a pilot who did rescues at sea. When the Persian Gulf War started, her ship headed to the Persian Gulf. She flew rescue missions and also flew food, ammunition, and medical equipment from supply ships to other Navy ships.

She never forgot her dream of driving a ship. When the rules changed so women could serve on combatant ships, she made her move. In the late 1990s, she was working as a helicopter pilot on a battleship. She obtained permission to train to be an OOD—"officer of the deck"—someone who helps drive the ship when the captain is off-duty. During her six months on that ship, she did all her flying duties and also practiced driving the ship under supervision until she could pass the test that's required before someone can be an official OOD. "After all those years, I was driving a warship! It's an incredible responsibility."

NAVY ELECTRICIAN'S MATE DIANNE RIVERA-JEAN (LEFT)
PREPARES TO DEPART IN LATE 1992 TO JOIN OTHER U.S.
TROOPS TAKING PART IN A UN PEACEKEEPING MISSION IN
THE AFRICAN COUNTRY OF SOMALIA.

8

KEEPING THE PEACE

1990s

"I always have the feeling that we as Americans should help where we can," said Lieutenant Colonel Christine Richardson. During the 1990s, the U.S. armed forces helped around the world by taking part in peacekeeping missions. Lieutenant Colonel Richardson served in one of them, in Bosnia. Fighting among warring groups in that Eastern European country had gone on for years. In 1995, the U.S. persuaded those groups to stop fighting. To be sure they did, the U.S. sent 20,000 troops to join a peacekeeping force run by NATO (North Atlantic Treaty Organization). European countries that were members of NATO also sent troops. She was there at the beginning of this mission to make sure U.S. Army troops were provided with the support they needed. This peacekeeping mission has continued for many years. All through the 1990s, U.S. forces also continued to patrol in the Persian Gulf area to keep the peace and make sure Iraq did what it promised to do in the agreement that ended the Persian Gulf War.

U.S. troops also joined another NATO mission in Kosovo, a region in a European country that used to be called Yugoslavia (now named Serbia and Montenegro). NATO tried to restore the peace there by persuading Yugoslav forces to stop their brutal attacks on certain groups in Kosovo. When that failed, the U.S. led a NATO effort in 1999 that bombed Yugoslavia until its troops left Kosovo. Air Force Colonel Kimberly Olson was put in charge of all the pilots who would do the midair refueling for this NATO mission. She had commanded an Air Force refueling squadron for several years, but this was different. On this NATO mission, she had to supervise the refueling of planes from 61 squadrons flying for 19 countries. With so many planes from so many countries needing in-the-sky refueling, she had to create a careful plan for how the refueling would be done in order to avoid accidents. From a command center at a base in Italy, she supervised thousands of refueling flights during her two-month mission. There were almost no "near misses"—times when planes almost hit.

Servicewomen took other steps forward during these missions. In 1994, for the first time Navy women were permanent crew members on a combatant ship in a war zone: About 400 women served side by side with more than a thousand men on the aircraft carrier USS *Eisenhower* in the Persian Gulf. In 1998, when officials feared that Iraq was making biological and chemical weapons, U.S. planes bombed places where Iraqis might be making those weapons. Navy Lieutenant Kendra Williams piloted one of those bombing missions, the first American woman to do so.

Women made major contributions to these missions, whether achieving firsts or not. Major General William Nash, head of U.S. forces in Bosnia, said, "In Bosnia, the performance of women was indistinguishable from that of their male counterparts. . . . whether turning a wrench in a muddy motor pool or standing guard at a base camp or flying a helicopter. Their intellect, their dedication were absolutely outstanding."

"We went into a port to load up on supplies and then would meet an aircraft carrier or other ship in the Mediterranean," said Lieutenant Commander Kristen Fabry. In the early 1990s, she worked on a Navy supply ship that provided food and spare parts to combatant ships keeping watch on Iraq as part of the peacekeeping mission in the Persian Gulf region. A strong wire would go from her supply ship to the other ship. Supplies would be hooked onto the wire and then would slide across the wire to the other ship. Or helicopters would fly supplies from her ship to the other one.

She graduated from the Naval Academy before women could serve on combatant ships. The first supply ships she served on had been built for all-male crews. They had been fixed up for women, but there were some problems. One ship had a big bathroom with lots of showers for male officers, but there was only a small, one-person bathroom for the five female officers. "There was a male engineer who used it, too. We'd get so angry. We'd be standing there in our bathrobes with our soap and shampoo, waiting to get in. So we figured out when he went in and set up times to get there first. One of us would be there at 6:30 a.m., and I'd come at 6:40, and someone else would come at 6:50. We were quick. We shut him out." After women were allowed on combatant ships, she served on new ships built with women in mind that had better bathrooms for females. Taking a shower wasn't such a hassle.

Later, after the Navy gave her time to earn a master's degree in business administration at a major university, she became a supply officer on the huge aircraft carrier USS *Abraham Lincoln,* a combatant ship with a crew of 5,500 sailors and aviators. In 2003, this ship took part in a second war in the Persian Gulf, the one that ended the rule of Iraqi dictator Saddam Hussein *(see Chapter 9).* She helped make sure there was enough food on the aircraft carrier and also kept the ship's stores, laundry, post office, and cash machines open and running.

AN UNPEACEFUL MISSION

One of the 1990s peacekeeping missions turned very unpeaceful. Thousands of people were starving in the African country of Somalia, partly because of too little rain, partly because of years of fighting among local Somali groups. In late 1992, the UN sent in a peacekeeping force made up of troops from the U.S. and other members of the UN. This UN force was supposed to provide security for organizations that were trying to distribute food to hungry people. But fighting started. Peacekeepers were attacked. "A truck convoy I led was fired on, probably by thugs trying to steal the supplies. We stopped, got out, and returned fire. I returned fire, too. Fortunately, they took off," said Captain Julie DelGiorno, who headed a transportation unit.

"We came under mortar attack the first night we were there," said Colonel Christine Knighton, an Army Black Hawk helicopter pilot. She commanded a unit that was usually based in Kentucky. It went to Somalia in 1993 to take over for troops who were finishing their tour of duty there. Troops usually go to danger zones for

A FEW YEARS AFTER SERVING IN SOMALIA, COLONEL CHRISTINE KNIGHTON COMMANDED A BATTALION THAT PROVIDED AVIATION SUPPORT FOR PEACEKEEPERS IN BOSNIA. BY THEN, SHE HAD A TWO-YEAR-OLD SON. HER HUSBAND, AN ARMY OFFICER, WAS ON SPECIAL ASSIGNMENT, SO THEIR SON STAYED WITH HIS GRAND-MOTHER FOR THE FOUR MONTHS HIS MOM WAS AWAY. SHE KEPT IN TOUCH BY PHONE AND BY USING SOMETHING NOT AVAILABLE TO TROOPS IN EARLIER WARS: E-MAIL.

a limited time. The troops who were leaving showed her the bunker holes they had dug for protection near their sleeping tents. The 150 members of her company used those bunkers a lot during their seven months in Somalia. "We were mortared every night," she recalled. The attacks did not kill anyone on the compound but damaged nearby helicopters. That meant more work for her unit, whose job it was to keep helicopters ready for action. She was the first female commander of this company. Most of its members were male, but she was used to leading the way, having been one of the first African-American women trained to be a military pilot.

Soon it was clear there was no peace to keep in Somalia, especially after 18 Army troops were brutally killed when their Black Hawk helicopter was shot down. The peacekeeping mission in Somalia was ended. The peacekeepers went home. In spite of this, Command Sergeant Major Cynthia Pritchett, who served in Somalia, felt the mission still managed to do "a lot of good things for a starving population."

COMBAT STRESS

During the mission in Somalia, Lieutenant Colonel E. Cameron Ritchie, an Army psychiatrist, was a member of a new kind of team that was being deployed for the first time: Combat Stress Teams. These teams could help troops cope better with what they might experience in such a dangerous situation. Besides psychiatrists, the teams could also include psychologists, chaplains, social workers, nurses, and medics. Commanders can have Combat Stress Teams talk with their troops after an upsetting event, such as a fellow soldier's death. "In talking with soldiers, we describe the kinds of things they might experience, like jitteriness or flashbacks," said Lieutenant Colonel Ritchie. "We explain that if you feel those things, that's normal. But if they bother you, come and talk to us one-on-one or with others in the group." These teams can also talk with soldiers who have other worries, such as about their families back home.

Command Sergeant Major Pritchett made sure Combat Stress Teams worked with her troops in Somalia. She was the top enlisted person in her battalion. She took care of the day-to-day supervision of the battalion's more than 900 soldiers. They often came under attack as they repaired roads or provided fuel and clean water for other peacekeepers. They worked in different areas of Mogadishu, the Somali capital. She drove each day to where they were to find out about difficulties they might be having. "I could have stayed at the base, but what kind of example would that have been for the soldiers? They needed to see me, as the leader, out and about," she said. Risking danger like that each day to help her troops on the streets of Mogadishu earned her a Bronze Star for "outstanding, caring leadership."

LIEUTENANT COLONEL ANITA DIXON

"When I got to Bosnia, the soldier who greeted me said, 'Ma'am, you need to lock and load your weapon.' The only time I could remember locking and loading a weapon was in training. But there were some people in Bosnia who were unhappy we were there," said Army Lieutenant Colonel Anita Dixon. Soon Bosnians realized that the peacekeepers were there to help. She did her part to win people over: "I gave candy to kids on the street."

She worked in the personnel department of the Army's First Armored Division, keeping track of the troops who were taking part in the Bosnia peacekeeping mission, "making sure the right people were in the right job at the right time. We coordinated with each base camp to see that they had who they needed." Moving to Bosnia and living in a tent for six months was hard, but she was used to moving. As a kid, she moved many times. Her dad was in the Army and the family went along whenever he took a job at a new Army post. She has moved a lot during her own Army career. She became an officer in 1985, right after college. "Your children have to sacrifice a lot for you when you are in the military," explained Lieutenant Colonel Dixon, a single mom. But there are benefits. Her teenage daughter, Brittni, speaks French and has friends around the world. During the Bosnia mission, Brittni stayed with her grandmother in Virginia. "That was tough. We e-mailed a lot," said Lieutenant Colonel Dixon. "It would be unusual for me to live in one place for more than four years. I've never done that. Moving is a way of life. Because I love what I do, I don't mind. It's good to know I'm doing something honorable for my country."

COMMAND SERGEANT MAJOR
CYNTHIA PRITCHETT IN HER
HUMVEE DURING THE MISSION
IN SOMALIA

ON THE MOVE

In addition to servicewomen's contributions to peacekeeping missions, there were other steps forward during the 1990s. At the start of the decade, Lieutenant Commander Darlene Iskra became the first woman to command a noncombat Navy ship. In 1998, Commander Maureen Farren became the first woman to command a different kind of ship: a combatant one. In 1995, Colonel Eileen Collins, an Air Force pilot and astronaut, became the first female to pilot the space shuttle. More military jobs opened up on the ground, too. By the end of the 1990s, servicewomen were able to try their hand at more than 90 percent of military jobs.

All through this decade, increasing numbers of minority women joined the force. By the end of the 1990s, African-American women made up just under half of the women in the Army and Navy. Nearly ten percent of Army and Navy women were Hispanic Americans. In 1995, the military promoted the first African-American woman to become a two-star general, Air Force Major General Marcelite Harris.

There was one development in the 1990s that was not so good: Officials began to admit that the armed forces had a sexual harassment problem. Newspapers reported incidents in which some military men had abused and sexually harassed military women. Officials took firm steps to try to put an end to that kind of behavior. There has been some improvement. Unfortunately, sexual harassment, although definitely against the rules, is a problem that has not completely gone away in the military or in the civilian world either.

On a more positive note, during this decade many squadrons had their first female commanders, such as Colonel Olson, who became the first female pilot to command the "Screaming Eagles," an Air Force squadron that refuels planes in the air. Usually based in Washington State, it went to Saudi Arabia for two months in 1997 to refuel planes patrolling over Iraq. As a mom, Colonel Olson knew how worried the parents of her 200 troops would be. She wrote to the parents. "I told them how proud they should be of their kid and thanked them for raising a child who would serve the nation," she said. "A lot of the time that was the first they had ever heard from the military. They would call their child and say, 'I got this great card from your commander and we're so proud of you.'" This helped build team spirit. So did her habit of spending time with the mechanics as they prepared planes for the next day's flying. Her team-building paid off. "We won a bunch of awards: best on-time record and best safety record."

Her husband helped, too. He took a few weeks off from his job as an airline pilot to stay home and take care of their two kids while she was away. He also looked out for the squadron's spouses, paying special attention to the 21 wives who were pregnant. Troops serving overseas like to know that someone is watching out for their families. "He's the squadron commander's spouse and that's part of the spouse's job," said Colonel Olson. That a husband would fill that role for his wife, the commander of an award-winning squadron, showed how much things were changing.

9

AFGHANISTAN, IRAQ, & BEYOND

"I lost a lot of friends and comrades that day," said Lieutenant Colonel Anita Dixon. She was working in Washington, D.C., on September 11, 2001. That's the day terrorists killed about 3,000 people by crashing hijacked planes into the World Trade Center in New York City, into a field in Pennsylvania, as well as into the west wall of the Pentagon, the armed forces headquarters that's just outside Washington. Although Lieutenant Colonel Dixon was based at the Pentagon then, she was out of the office that morning, working on a special project. However, people she usually worked with were among the 184 who died at the Pentagon. Ten servicewomen lost their lives.

Servicewomen were not just victims that day. They were also rescuers. Navy Lieutenant Antonia Lopez, a physician's assistant, ran to the crash site as soon as the plane hit the Pentagon. She and Army doctor Captain Theresa Nguyen were among the many military healthcare workers who stayed at the crash site until late in the night, treating people injured in the attack as well as firefighters who battled the blaze caused by the crash. Women were also in National Guard units that protected U.S. cities, airports, train stations, landmarks, power plants, and ports to prevent more attacks. Lieutenant Junior Grade Dawn Prebula served on a Coast Guard ship that patrolled the nation's eastern coast.

A month later, the U.S., Britain, and several other countries struck back in Afghanistan against terrorists responsible for the September 11 attacks. U.S. women were part of the action, performing a wide range of important jobs. They were among the pilots who flew planes that dropped food packages for the Afghan people. Female sailors helped run the aircraft carriers from which other female pilots took off in planes to carry out combat missions. Women Marines were among the troops that went into Afghanistan. Several servicewomen lost their lives, including Sergeant Jeannette Winters, a Marine radio operator, who died when the plane she was on crashed in Pakistan. She was the first female Marine to die in a war zone.

Then in 2003, women were part of the huge force that took part in another war—in Iraq. The U.S., Britain, and other countries sent troops to free Iraq from the rule of dictator Saddam Hussein and to prevent Iraq from using weapons of mass destruction, such as ones with deadly chemicals. Although servicewomen were not allowed to take part in direct combat on the ground, many served in support units that traveled into Iraq with infantry divisions. Some women were injured and taken prisoner. Specialist Lori Piestewa lost her life when her unit was ambushed.

As new conflicts arise at home or abroad, servicewomen will continue to play a role. Command Sergeant Major Mary Sutherland noted, "It takes something like September 11th to raise people's awareness of the military. But, hey, we were here on September 10th too. It's something the American people take for granted, that we're there doing what we do so they can have peace."

MAKING A DIFFERENCE

"You felt you were making a difference. We saw pictures of kids picking up the food packets, and we knew we were the ones who put the stuff there," said Captain Elizabeth Dunn. This Air Force pilot flew planes that dropped food packets over Afghanistan during the start of Operation Enduring Freedom, as the mission there was called. Dropping those food packets was tricky. The C-17 jet she flew was designed for delivering troops and supplies. Usually, to make a delivery, the jet would swoop down low. Then crew members would open the back door and troops could parachute out. Or the jet would land so supplies like tanks, trucks, and helicopters could be unloaded. But because she was dropping those food packets at the very start of the mission in Afghanistan, it was too risky to swoop down low or land. People shooting from the ground might hit her plane. To stay out of their range, she had to keep the plane up so high that it lost pressure when its back door opened to let the food packets drop. Loss of pressure made it hard to breathe. "We had to put on our oxygen masks," she said. "I'm an airdrop pilot and we practice drops all the time, but not that high." This was a first.

After a few weeks, the food drops ended. Then she delivered troops and equipment to Afghanistan, usually taking off from bases in Turkey or Europe. So did Captain Erin Rickenbacker, who noted, "It was scary flying where people are shooting at you." Captain Dunn added, "You never know what will happen. Flying is hours of boredom interrupted by a few seconds of sheer terror. But you level your mind, relax, and it all comes through."

Navy Hospital Corpsman Melinda Scruggs was too busy to feel scared during the fighting in Afghanistan.

AFGHAN CHILDREN (BELOW) GATHER SOME OF THE FOOD PACKETS DROPPED BY U.S. PLANES. CAPTAIN ELIZABETH DUNN (INSET) IS AT THE CONTROLS OF A C-17, THE KIND OF JET SHE FLEW OVER AFGHANISTAN TO DROP FOOD PACKETS. EVER SINCE SHE WAS A LITTLE GIRL, SHE HAS BEEN FASCINATED BY PLANES. "ONE OF THE COOLEST THINGS IS FLYING AT NIGHT AND LOOKING AT ALL THE STARS AROUND YOU. ONE DAY WE SAW THE SUN SETTING ON ONE SIDE OF THE PLANE AND THE MOON RISING ON THE OTHER."

She was the commander of an all-male platoon that built and ran the first clinic at a new Marine base in Kandahar, Afghanistan. Living conditions were rough, with no showers or hot food. Her clinic treated injured Marines and Afghans. "You realize they're firing at you, but you get into the mind-set of, 'OK, what do we need to do now?' You don't think about what could happen to you."

Supplies used in building that clinic were there thanks partly to Captain Hilary Williams, the Marine supply officer for three Navy supply ships. Marines do not have ships of their own but travel on Navy ships. Small landing boats launched from those ships bring Marines and supplies ashore. "We parked in front of Pasni, Pakistan, set up a beach landing site, and off-loaded supplies: tanks, trucks, water purification systems, paper, food, lumber, building materials, wire, engine oil, and more," she explained. She stayed on shore a few nights to supervise the unloading of supplies, which were then flown to Afghanistan. Mostly, she was at a command center on shipboard to receive messages about other supplies troops needed in Afghanistan. She would then contact supply bases in the U.S., Europe, and the Middle East to find the supplies. Navy ships brought the supplies to her. "We met the ships at sea and they would helicopter the supplies to our ship. It was awesome. You had to have an 'I can do it' attitude every day. My job never ended. We always needed more stuff. It was hard but I liked the leadership responsibility."

One result of Operation Enduring Freedom was the new hope given to Afghan women. U.S.-led forces ended the rule of a group called the Taliban, which had supported the terrorist group responsible for the September 11 attack on the U.S. Under Taliban rule, girls could not go to school. Women could not vote, have jobs, or receive good medical care. After Taliban rule ended in late 2001, girls headed to school for the first time in many years. Other opportunities began opening for Afghan women.

INTO IRAQ ONCE MORE

About a year after the start of the Afghan mission, a serious problem cropped up that was left over from the Persian Gulf War. As part of the agreement ending that earlier war, Iraq was supposed to destroy its weapons of mass destruction. In November 2002, the UN said Iraq had to prove it had finally done so. By early 2003, the governments of the U.S., Great Britain, and some other nations felt Iraqi dictator Saddam Hussein had no plans to obey that order. In March 2003, more than 100,000 troops from the U.S., Britain, Australia, and several other countries invaded Iraq to free its people from this dictator and his brutal regime. In less than a month, his rule ended.

American servicewomen played a major role. Captain Dunn flew in troops, vehicles, and supplies, as she had in Afghanistan. "At first, we flew into Iraq at night under the cover of darkness, flying and landing while wearing Night Vision Goggles, allowing us to see in the dark," she said. Many other women, like Army Sergeant Jennifer Raichle, served in the Iraqi desert with the fighting forces. She was an intelligence analyst for the Third Infantry Division. Her job was to learn all she could about Iraq's fighters, to figure out what their plans might be. Other servicewomen repaired and refueled vehicles in Iraq, operated communications equipment, and gave medical care. Air Force Colonel Kimberly Olson was chosen to work with a team of experts and officials to help the Iraqi people set up a new government after the fighting ended.

Hundreds of women also served on combatant ships in the waters near Iraq. "Women worked in virtually every area on our ship," noted Navy Lieutenant Commander Kristen Fabry. She served on a Navy aircraft carrier, the USS *Abraham Lincoln,* helping to make sure that this nuclear-powered floating airport had enough supplies. "Although there were only about 500

SPECIALIST LORI PIESTEWA

The Army unit in which Specialist Lori Piestewa served was not a combat outfit, but it came under fire early in the March 2003 invasion of Iraq. She was a member of a maintenance company, made up of young men and women who were mechanics, supply clerks, and cooks. They repaired military vehicles and provided other support for the fighting force. Her unit's trucks followed behind the combat tanks across the Iraqi desert. The tanks were supposed to clear away enemy troops so support units would not be in danger. But the trucks and Humvees in her unit were attacked by Iraqi fighters. Maintenance units have some weapons, but not enough to fight off such an attack. When U.S. troops arrived to help, they discovered that some in her unit had survived, some had been killed, but several were missing, including Specialist Piestewa and two other women.

Her friend and roommate, Private First Class Jessica Lynch, was rescued in a nighttime raid on the Iraqi hospital where she had been taken. There, rescuers found the bodies of several other members of the maintenance company, including Specialist Piestewa's. The other missing servicewoman, Specialist Shoshana Johnson, had been taken prisoner and was found, a few weeks later—injured but alive—with other soldiers who had been taken prisoner.

Specialist Piestewa was 23 years old when she died in this war, a single mother of two young children who were home in Arizona, being cared for by her parents. She was a Hopi, the first Native-American servicewoman to be killed in combat in a foreign war. Before her unit left the U.S. to go to Iraq, a newspaper photographer took this picture of her (above right) helping another soldier who was also on her way to serve in Iraq, Specialist Yesi Imperial. After learning of Specialist Piestewa's death, her brother told reporters, "Our family is proud of her. She is our hero.... She will not be forgotten." Arizona's female governor tried to make sure this servicewoman would be remembered. The governor proposed changing the name of a mountain in Arizona. Its old name was Squaw Peak, which Native Americans had long found insulting. Its new name: Piestewa Peak.

women in the crew of 5,500, there was almost no area where women were not working side by side with males. We had women pilots flying helicopters and jets, as well as working on airplanes as jet mechanics, electronic technicians, and parachute riggers. Women were 'shooters,' who helped planes take off from the flight deck by launching them from catapults. The most senior enlisted person in the Air Wing was a woman, as was the head of the Maintenance Department." Women also worked in engineering and served as Officer of the Deck (OOD),

helping to drive the "Abe" (the ship's nickname) when the captain was off duty. In addition, women made up nearly half the officers who ran the ship's nuclear power plant. "Life onboard a carrier is a team effort," she added. "It makes no difference what color, gender, ethnic background, or religious preference the person next to you possesses. Despite the extended period away from friends and loved ones, I'm glad I did not miss the opportunity to be there and do my part in Operation Iraqi Freedom."

SPECIALIST SHOSHANA JOHNSON (RIGHT), AN ARMY COOK AND MOTHER OF A TWO-YEAR-OLD, IS SHOWN HERE WITH SPECIALIST JOSEPH HUDSON AS THEY WAVE TO WELL-WISHERS AT THEIR HOME BASE IN TEXAS IN APRIL 2003. THEY HAD JUST RETURNED FROM IRAQ, WHERE THEY HAD BEEN HELD AS POWS FOR SEVERAL WEEKS. SHE WAS INJURED AND TAKEN PRISONER ALONG WITH SEVERAL OTHERS DURING AN ATTACK ON HER MAINTENANCE UNIT, THE SAME UNIT IN WHICH SPECIALIST PIESTEWA AND PRIVATE FIRST CLASS LYNCH SERVED.

A CHANCE TO SERVE

Women join the military today for many of the same reasons that women signed up in earlier times: to serve their country, tackle new challenges, and have an adventure. These days, some people also sign up as a way of finding a good job or having help paying for a college education. Corporal Hilda Brinson has taken several college courses paid for by the Marines since she enlisted, even taking a college math course taught by an officer on her ship while it was docked off the coast of Pakistan during the fighting in Afghanistan. Lieutenant Colonel E. Cameron Ritchie took part in an Army program that would pay her medical school bills if she promised to serve in the Army for four years after becoming a doctor. She has stayed in much longer than the required four years because the Army keeps giving her interesting new assignments.

The variety of opportunities attracts many other women as well. Commander Susan Fink has done a lot of things besides fly helicopters in her more than 15 years in the Navy. In addition to learning to drive a ship during one flying assignment (see Chapter 7), she has also spent a year earning a master's degree, another year working as a special military person assigned to the White House, and two years at a major university earning a Ph.D. degree in international relations. Colonel Christine Knighton, who has worked for the secretary of defense in addition to flying Black Hawk helicopters, explained that "I like being a leader, having the opportunity to work with young enlisted soldiers who want to make something of themselves. I stay in because I love what I'm doing." So does Command Sergeant Major Sutherland, who has been in the Army for more than 30 years: "I like being part of something big that makes a difference."

Not everyone stays in that long. Some grow tired of moving from base to base every few years or of being sent to danger zones and not seeing their families. Others, like Captain Julie DelGiorno, decide it's time for something new. After nine years in the Army, she left to be a college basketball coach and then a college administrator, noting that "I probably have my job today because of the skills I learned in the Army, the leadership skills, the organizational skills, being able to handle a lot of tasks at once."

None of these women chose to serve in the armed forces because they had a fondness for war. As Captain Celia FlorCruz observed after serving in the Persian Gulf War, "Nobody who has ever seen war would ever want anybody else to have to experience that." Men who have seen combat often feel that way, too. General Douglas MacArthur, one of the chief commanders in World War II, said that "the soldier above all other people prays for peace, for he must suffer and bear the deepest wounds and scars of war." But, as Captain FlorCruz added, "You need to keep the military strong to protect our freedom and our safety." Commander Lura Emery, a Navy nurse who served in Korea, explained her feelings this way: "I detest war. But if it comes to our freedom, we have no alternative." She added, "Like it or not…we have to fight for our freedom."

YOU'VE COME A LONG WAY

Servicewomen have come a long way from the days when they had to disguise themselves as men to defend the nation. Today, about 14 percent of people in the U.S. armed forces are female—one out of every seven. Nearly 200,000 servicewomen are on active duty, with about 130,000 in the Reserves or National Guard. More than 90 percent of military careers are open to them, a higher percentage than in most countries. As Army doctor Colonel Rhonda Cornum noted, "The qualities that are most important in all military jobs—things like integrity, moral courage and determination—have nothing to do with gender."

Women have also come a long way outside the military. In every year since 1983, more women than men have enrolled in colleges and universities. By the start of the 21st century, more than half of all women, including moms, were working, doing things like running huge corporations, performing brain surgery, working at construction sites, playing pro basketball, and serving in Congress. "There's nothing women can't do if they set their minds to it," observed Lieutenant Commander Fabry. But some women still run into the situation faced by servicewomen in the past: having to prove they're tough enough for the job. This can happen in the civilian world—and in the military, too. As one servicewoman put it, the military is "still a male-run organization, I kid you not." Although the percentage of servicewomen is rising, most military people are male. "But once you prove yourself, you're accepted. It's something you have to work through. I don't let it get me down," said Command Sergeant Major Cynthia Pritchett.

Sometimes Air Force pilot Captain Dunn lands at bases where people don't know her. When she climbs out of the cockpit, some men look puzzled. "They ask, 'Where's the pilot?' And I say, 'I'm, like, right here.' I've learned to joke about it." When she flies with a female co-pilot, people in her squadron joke that it's an "unmanned cockpit." But mostly, she feels accepted as "just one of the guys."

"We are lucky to have a lot of men in the military who see the value of women," said Colonel Kimberly Olson. She is grateful to male commanders who had enough confidence in her to pick her for important positions. However, she also feels the military is lucky to have more and more women participating in making decisions. "Women often see the world differently from men and it makes for a better team to have women sitting at the table."

WOMEN HAVE SHOWN THEY CAN HANDLE THE STRESS OF MILITARY WORK, INCLUDING THE STRESS OF BASIC TRAINING. IN MOST PARTS OF THE MILITARY, WOMEN AND MEN GO THROUGH BASIC TRAINING TOGETHER. THIS NEW FEMALE ARMY RECRUIT (FRONT OF LINE) IS MARCHING RIGHT ALONG WITH THE NEW MALE RECRUITS IN HER BASIC TRAINING UNIT.

RESOURCES

Few books have been written for young people on women in the military. However there are some for adults that a motivated young reader might find fascinating. Here are the main books I read in doing research. Those with an asterisk are written for kids.

BIOGRAPHIES AND AUTOBIOGRAPHIES OF PEOPLE FEATURED IN THIS BOOK:

Alcott, Louisa May. *Hospital Sketches.* Boston: J. Redpath, 1863. Reissued. Bedford, Mass.: Applewood Books, 1993.

Bigler, Philip. *Hostile Fire: The Life and Death of First Lieutenant Sharon Lane.* Arlington, Va.: Vandamere Press, 1996.

Brion, Irene. *Lady GI: A Woman's War in the South Pacific.* Novato, Calif.: Presidio, 1997.

Burgess, Lauren Cook. *An Uncommon Soldier.* New York: Oxford University Press, 1994.

Claghorn, Charles. *Women Patriots of the American Revolution. A Biographical Dictionary.* Metuchen, N.J.: Scarecrow Press, 1991.

Cornum, Rhonda. *She Went to War: The Rhonda Cornum Story.* Novato, Calif.: Presidio Press, 1992.

Earley, Charity Adams. *One Woman's Army: A Black Officer Remembers the WAC.* College Station, Tex.: Texas A&M University Press, 1989.

Gunter, Helen Clifford. *Navy Wave: Memories of World War II.* Fort Bragg, Calif.: Cypress House Press, 1992.

Holland, Mary Gardner, ed. *Our Army Nurses.* Boston, Mass.: B. Wilkins and Co., 1895, 1897. Reissued. Introduction by Daniel John Hoisington, Roseville, Minn.: Edinborough Press, 1998.

Hunton, Addie W. and Kathryn M. Johnson. *Two Colored Women with the American Expeditionary Forces.* Brooklyn, N.Y.: Brooklyn Eagle Press, 1920. Reissued. Introduction by Adele Logan Alexander. New York: G.K. Hall & Co., 1997

Oates, Stephen B. *A Woman of Valor: Clara Barton and the Civil War.* New York: The Free Press, 1994.

Powell, Colin L. with Joseph E. Persico. *My American Journey.* New York: Random House, 1995.

Pryor, Elizabeth Brown. *Clara Barton: Professional Angel.* Philadelphia: University of Pennsylvania Press, 1987.

Pullman, Sally Hitchcock. *Letters Home: Memoirs of One Army Nurse in the Southwest Pacific in World War II.* Granby, Conn.: Olivieri, Quickprint Centers, 1998.

Ryan, David D., ed. *A Yankee Spy in Richmond: The Civil War Diary of "Crazy Bet" Van Lew.* Mechanicsburg, Pa.: Stackpole Books, 1996.

Snyder, Charles McCool. *Dr. Mary Walker: The Little Lady in Pants.* New York: Arno Press, 1974.

Stimson, Julia C. *Finding Themselves: The Letters of an American Army Chief Nurse in a British Hospital in France.* New York: The Macmillan Company, 1918.

Taylor, Susie King. *Reminiscences of My Life in Camp with the 33rd United States Colored Troops.* Boston: S.K. Taylor, 1902. Reissued. *A Black Woman's Civil War Memoirs.* Patricia W. Romer, ed. Introduction by Willie Lee Rose. New York: Markus Wiener Publishing, 1988.

*Wachs, Eleanor. *Deborah Sampson Gannett: America's First Woman Soldier, A Source Booklet.* Boston: The Commonwealth Museum, 1997.

OTHER BOOKS:

Blanton, DeAnne and Lauren M. Cook. *They Fought Like Demons: Women Soldiers in the American Civil War.* Baton Rouge, La.: Louisiana State University Press, 2002.

Cayton, Mary Kupiec, Elliott J. Gorn, Peter W. Williams, eds. *Encyclopedia of American Social History.* New York: Charles Scribner's Sons, 1993.

*Colman, Penny. *Rosie the Riveter: Women Working on the Home Front in World War II.* New York: Crown Publishers, 1995.

De Pauw, Linda Grant. *Battle Cries and Lullabies: Women in War From Prehistory to the Present.* Norman, Okla.: University of Oklahoma Press, 1998.

Ebbert, Jean and Marie-Beth Hall. *Crossed Currents: Navy Women from WWI to Tailhook.* New York: Brassey's (US), 1993; 3rd edition, 1999.

Ebbert, Jean and Marie-Beth Hall. *The First, the Few, the Forgotten: Navy and Marine Corps Women in World War I.* Annapolis, Md.: Naval Institute Press, 2002.

Evans, Elizabeth. *Weathering the Storm: Women of the American Revolution.* New York: Encore Editions, 1975.

Feller, Carolyn M. and Constance J. Moore, eds. *Highlights in the History of the Army Nurse Corps.* Washington, D.C.: U.S. Army Center of Military History, 1995.

Francke, Linda Bird. *Ground Zero: The Gender Wars in the Military.* New York: Simon and Schuster, 1997.

Gavin, Lettie. *American Women in World War I: They Also Served.* Niwot, Colo: University of Colorado Press, 1997.

*Hakim, Joy. *A History of Us* (Books One to Ten). New York: Oxford University Press, 1993.

Hewitt, Linda. *Women Marines in World War I.* Washington, D.C.: History and Museums Division, Headquarters, U.S. Marine Corps, 1974.

Holm, Jeanne M., editor. *In Defense of a Nation: Servicewomen in World War II.* Washington, D.C.: Vandamere Press, 1998.

Holm, Jeanne. *Women in the Military: An Unfinished Revolution.* Novato, Calif.: Presidio Press, 1982; revised edition, 1992.

*Hoose, Phillip. *We Were There, Too! Young People in U.S. History.* New York: Farrar Straus Giroux, 2001.

Leonard, Elizabeth. *All the Daring of the Soldier: Women of the Civil War Armies.* New York: W.W. Norton & Co., 1999.

Lewis, Vickie. *Side-by-Side: A Photographic History of American Women in War.* New York: Stewart, Tabori and Chang, 1999.

Moore, Brenda L. *To Serve My Country, to Serve My Race: The Story of the Only African American WACs Stationed Overseas During World War II.* New York: New York University Press, 1996.

*Nathan, Amy. *Yankee Doodle Gals: Women Pilots of World War II.* Washington, D.C.: National Geographic Society, 2001.

Norman, Elizabeth M. *We Band of Angels: The Untold Story of American Nurses Trapped on Bataan by the Japanese.* New York: Pocket Books, 1999.

Norman, Elizabeth M. *Women at War: The Story of Fifty Military Nurses Who Served in Vietnam.* Philadelphia, Pa.; University of Pennsylvania Press, 1990.

Omori, Frances. *Quiet Heroes: Navy Nurses of the Korean War 1950-1953 Far East Command.* Saint Paul, Minn.: Smith House Press, 2000.

Quarles, Benjamin. *The Negro in the Civil War.* Boston: Little, Brown and Company, 1969.

Sterner, Doris M. *In and Out of Harm's Way: A History of the Navy Nurse Corps.* Seattle, Wash.: Peanut Butter Publishing, 1997.

Tierney, Helen. *Women's Studies Encyclopedia.* New York: Greenwood Press, 1989.

Vaught, Wilma L. *The Day the Nation Said "Thanks!": A History and Dedication Scrapbook of the Women in Military Service for America Memorial.* Washington, D.C.: Military Women's Press, 1999.

Walker, Keith. *A Piece of My Heart: The Stories of Twenty-Six Women Who Served in Vietnam.* Novato, Calif.: Presidio Press, 1985.

Weatherford, Doris. *American Women and World War II.* New York: Facts on File, 1990.

Woolsey, Jane Stuart. *Hospital Days: Reminiscence of a Civil War Nurse.* Roseville, Minn. Edinborough Press, 1996.

VIDEO

Korean War Stories. Robert Uth, producer/director. Walter Cronkite, narrator. PBS Home Video, 2001.

WEB SITES

http://www.womensmemorial.org

http://userpages.aug.com/captbarb/

http://www.defenselink.mil/

http://www.loc.gov/folklife/vets/vets-home.html

http://www.awm.lee.army.mil/

QUOTE NOTES

(See Bibliography for full bibliographic information)

Quotes from Frieda Mae Hardin and from Colonel Rhonda Cornum's daughter can be found in Wilma L. Vaught's *The Day the Nation Said "Thanks!"* The quote from Colonel Mary Hallaren in the Introduction appears in the Women's Memorial 2000 calendar; her quote in Chapter 4 appears in Jeanne M. Holm's *In Defense of a Nation.* The quote from Secretary Colin Powell comes from his autobiography, *My American Journey.* Quotes from Louisa May Alcott, Lieutenant Colonel Charity Adams Earley, Lieutenant Helen Clifford Gunter, Addie W. Hunton, First Lieutenant Sally Hitchcock Pullman, Julia C. Stimson, and Susie King Taylor come from the books they wrote. Some quotes from Corporal Irene Brion come from her memoir, *Lady GI;* others come from a telephone interview conducted by the author. Quotes from Sarah Rosetta Wakeman come from letters she wrote that were published in 1994 in Lauren Cook Burgess's *An Uncommon Soldier.* Quotes from Matilda Morris, Harriet Scott, Helen Smith, and Elizabeth Wheeler come from Mary Gardner Holland's *Our Army Nurses;* the quote from Dorothea Dix appears in the 1998 reprinting of that book. Quotes about Annie Etheridge come from Elizabeth Leonard's *All the Daring of the Soldier.* Quotes from Sergeant Martha Wilchinski and Private First Class Edith Macias appear in Linda Hewitt's *Women Marines in World War I.* The quote from the Navy nurse at the start of Chapter 4 appears in Doris M. Sterner's *In and Out of Harm's Way.* Quotes from a WAC (Chapter 6), from Captain Cynthia Mosley, and Major Marie T. Rossi appear in Jeanne Holm's *Women in the Military.* The quote from Aileen Cole Stewart comes from an article she wrote in *The American Journal of Nursing,* vol. 63, no. 9, September 1963. Quotes from Grace Banker Paddock come from an article she wrote, published in *Yankee Magazine* in March 1974. The brief excerpt from one of Laura Frost Smith's World War I letters appeared in an article in the *Seattle Post-Intelligencer,* September 24, 1998. Quotes from Deborah Samson come from a book written about her in 1797 by Hermann Mann, parts of which were reprinted in Elizabeth Evans', *Weathering the Storm.* Quotes from Rose Heavren, Lillian Blackwell Dial, Helen Fairchild, and Loretta Walsh come from materials in the archives of the Women's Memorial, including unpublished memoirs and letters. Most quotes from Commander Lura Emery and Captain Carmela Filosa Hix come from telephone interviews conducted by the author; a few come from transcripts of interviews conducted by the Disabled American Veterans Foundation. The quote from General Douglas MacArthur was supplied by Dr. Stephen Grove, West Point historian.

Quotes from other servicewomen and veterans come from interviews conducted by the author.

ACKNOWLEDGMENTS

I am very grateful to Brigadier General Wilma Vaught, president of the Women In Military Service For America Memorial Foundation, Inc., and members of her staff who have been so helpful in all stages of this project, especially Dr. Judith Bellafaire, the memorial's historian, and Britta Granrud, the memorial's curator, both of whom were very generous with their time and gave suggestions of books to read, experts to contact, and veterans to interview. They gave me access to unpublished memoirs and letters, as well as articles, photographs, and other materials in their archives; they also reviewed the book's manuscript, offering valuable suggestions. Additional thanks for many helpful suggestions go to two other military historians: Dr. Gina Akers, Naval Historical Center; and Constance A. Burns, Curator, Military History, and specialist in minority and African-American history at the U.S. Army Center of Military History.

In addition, I am extremely grateful to the veterans and active-duty servicewomen whom I interviewed by phone. I feel honored that these remarkable women were willing to share their experiences and their personal photos: First Lieutenant Lily Lee Adams, Colonel Margaret Bailey, Captain Julia Barnes, Corporal Hilda Brinson, Corporal Traycee Brinson, Corporal Irene Brion, Staff Sergeant Kim Chambers, First Lieutenant Dorothy Steinbis Davis, First Lieutenant Evelyn Decker, Captain Julie DelGiorno, Lieutenant Colonel Anita Dixon, Captain Elizabeth Dunn, Commander Lura Emery, Lieutenant Commander Kristen Fabry, Commander Susan Fink, Captain Celia FlorCruz, Chief Petty Officer Mary Fowlkes, Captain Carmela Filosa Hix, First Lieutenant Mikie Keck, Colonel Christine Knighton, Captain Christina Richter Listermann, Lieutenant Antonia Lopez, Major Nora Marcos, Captain Theresa Nguyen, Colonel Kimberly Olson, Lieutenant jg Dawn Prebula, Command Sergeant Major Cynthia Pritchett, First Lieutenant Sally Hitchcock Pullman, Lieutenant Colonel Christine Richardson, Captain Erin Rickenbacker, Lieutenant Colonel E. Cameron Ritchie, HMC Melinda Scruggs, Command Sergeant Major Mary Sutherland, Staff Sergeant Ernestine Johnson Thomas, Captain Hilary Williams, Private First Class Muriel Wimmer, and Commander Lucy Young. Thanks also go to Erika Adams, daughter of Lieutenant Lily Lee Adams; Mary Budds, niece of Rose Heavren; Captain Jerald Kirsten, son of Frieda Mae Hardin; Helen Richardson, niece of Lieutenant Helen Clifford Gunter; Nelle Rote, niece of Helen Fairchild; Ruth Talbert, daughter of Lilliann Blackwell Dial; and Grace Timbie, daughter of Grace Banker Paddock.

Also supportive and helpful were people in the public affairs offices or historical departments of the military who answered my many questions and put me in touch with veterans and active-duty people to interview: Army—Captain Deanna Bague, Lieutenant Colonel Margaret Flott, Major Linda Guardado-McRandal, Dr. Betty Maxfield, Jean Offut, Martha Rudd, Terri Sirois, Rebecca Smith;

Navy—Lieutenant Kathleen Sandoz, André B. Sobocinski, Lieutenant Jon Spiers; Marines—Captain James Jarvis, Sergeant Esther Maysonet, and Lance Corporal Carl Schnaufer; Air Force—Lieutenant Jennifer Andrews, Lieutenant Colonel Ed Memi, Second Lieutenant Brandon Pollachek; Coast Guard—Ed Kruska. Thanks also to John H. Greenwood, Chief of the Office of Medical History of the Surgeon General; Dr. Stephen Grove, West Point's historian; Dan Philbin, Office of the Assistant Secretary of Defense; and Sue Ketterer of West Point's Association of Graduates.

I would also like to thank historian Alfred Young, for his insights on Deborah Samson; historian Dr. Linda Grant De Pauw, who shared her views on Molly Pitcher; Dr. Elizabeth Norman, who gave me an overview of military nursing; historian Richard Miller, who spoke with me about African-American Yeomen (F); and David E. Autry of the Disabled American Veterans Foundation who provided transcripts of interviews as well as a copy of *Korean War Stories*. I am also grateful to Marlene Adler; Jerry G. Burgess, Director of the U.S. Army Women's Museum; Brigadier General Rosetta Y. Burke; Lieutenant Colonel Marilla Cushman; editor Suzanne Fonda; David Jackson, Defend America; research assistant Cheryl Klopfenstein; Teresita Kopka; Tammy Martin, Oberlin College Archives; Major Bonnie O'Leary; Shirely Schofield, Sharon, MA, Historical Society; Jenny Schuck; Shawna Shepherd; librarian Rachelle Shollenberger; Carol Smith; Colonel James Stokes; author Lauren Cook Wike; Lieutenant Colonel Betty Jane Williams; Anthony Wonderly, Oneida Indian Nation; and photographers Elvert X. Barnes, Marshall Karesh, Carolou Marquet, and James Singewald. Special thanks go to author Jean Ebbert, historian Elizabeth Leonard, and social studies teacher Denis O'Rourke for reviewing the manuscript and offering valuable advice. Thanks also to Judy Woodruff for spending time reviewing the manuscript and offering such warm words of support. I am also very grateful to Walter Cronkite for taking time out of his busy schedule to share his memories in the Foreword. Of course, I am also very thankful for the support and encouragement of my family: Carl, Eric, and Noah Nathan.

INDEX